CULTURES OF THE WORLD

NIGERIA

Patricia Levy

MARSHALL CAVENDISH
New York • London • Sydney

Reference edition published 1993 by
Marshall Cavendish Corporation
2415 Jerusalem Avenue
P.O. Box 587
North Bellmore
New York 11710

© Times Editions Pte Ltd 1993

Originated and designed by
Times Books International, an imprint of
Times Editions Pte Ltd

Printed in Singapore

Library of Congress Cataloging-in-Publication Data:
Levy, Patricia Marjorie,
   Nigeria / Patricia Levy.
     p. cm.—(Cultures Of The World)
   Includes bibliographical references and index.
   Summary: Describes the geography, history,
government, economy, and culture of Nigeria.
   ISBN 1-85435-574-0
   1. Nigeria—Juvenile literature [1. Nigeria.]
I. Title. II. Series.
DT515.22.L54 1993
966.9—dc20   92–38754
              CIP
               AC

Cultures of the World

Editorial Director	Shirley Hew
Managing Editor	Shova Loh
Editors	Leonard Lau
	Tan Kok Eng
	Michael Spilling
	Sue Sismondo
Picture Editor	Yee May Kaung
Production	Edmund Lam
Design	Tuck Loong
	Ronn Yeo
	Felicia Wong
	Loo Chuan Ming
Illustrators	Jimmy Kang
	Kelvin Sim
	Philip Lim
MCC Editorial Director	Evelyn M. Fazio

INTRODUCTION

PRESENT-DAY NIGERIA is a modern creation. It is composed of a variety of tribal groups and cultures brought together by the accident of colonial policy. As the largest and technically the wealthiest country in West Africa, it has the potential to be the most powerful nation in this part of the world. Oil has been the key to Nigeria's wealth, as well as the cause of many of its problems. Culturally, the country has rich and diverse traditions, and it has produced world-famous writers, athletes, artists, and dance troupes.

This book, part of the *Cultures of the World* series, provides the reader with an inside knowledge of how the people of Nigeria live, work, eat, and play. It offers insights into the values, beliefs, and customs of these lively and forward-looking people.

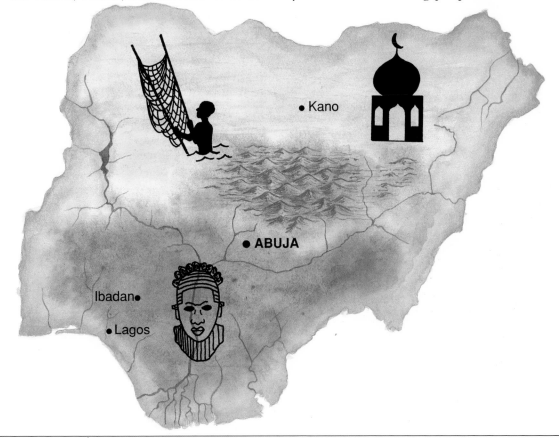

CONTENTS

A northern Nigerian tribesman, covered to protect against the heat of the sun.

CONTENTS

A corridor of an old-style Yoruba compound.

GEOGRAPHY

NIGERIA HAS EXISTED as an independent state for more than 30 years. It is one of the most dynamic and diverse of Africa's many varied states. With a total of 88.5 million people, it is the most densely populated of Africa's nations. It is also probably the wealthiest, having oil, tin, rubber, and other commodities as its principal exports. Nigeria's land mass covers an area roughly the size of California, Arizona, and New Mexico combined—around 356,669 square miles. The vegetation is of a wide variety of types, ranging from tropical rain forest to desert.

Nigeria's population is largely rural, but increasing numbers of people now see the cities as their means to a better life. Nigeria's people are divided into many tribes with as many languages. The principal languages are Hausa, Yoruba, and Ibo, with English as the commonly used and official language.

Opposite: **A village in the northern Nigerian region of Borno, near Maiduguri.**

Left: **Mangrove swamps in the Niger Delta, southern Nigeria.**

EROSION

One consequence of Nigeria's heavy rainfall is erosion. There are some spectacular examples of this on the Jos Plateau, where 4,800 miles of gullies caused by erosion have been counted, with an estimated 1 million tons of soil moved. In the south, in areas where the rain forest has been cleared, whole hillsides have disappeared. Eroded soil deposited in the rivers is highly fertile, and for the season that it lies in the dried up river beds it can be cultivated. The following rainy season brings new soil deposits. Farmers along some river banks need never worry about soil fertility, but this is at the cost of rain forests and massive erosion.

An example of erosion near Enugu in southern Nigeria.

PHYSICAL FEATURES

Nigeria has coastline on the Gulf of Guinea and borders Benin to the west and Cameroon to the east. To the north are Niger and Chad.

Nigeria is divided into three neat sections by the Niger and Benue rivers, which join in the center of the country before flowing down to the Niger Delta.

The coastline is sheltered from the ravages of the open sea by a narrow belt of coastal swamps, lagoons, and creeks. North of the coast, the mangrove swamps give way to tropical rain forest. Farther north still, there is the savanna, and at its northernmost extremities, the desolation of the desert.

CLIMATE

With its tropical climate, Nigeria does not experience the seasons typical of a climate such as found in the United States. It does, however, have seasons of a kind, determined by global air movements.

A dry air mass over the Sahara Desert to the north and a moist air mass from the south Atlantic meet over Nigeria and form bands of weather that move as the year progresses. Between December and March, the dry air mass is strong and dominates the whole country, bringing drought to northern Nigeria. At this time the south has little rainfall.

The point where the two air masses meet moves northward in April, so the south experiences heavy tropical rainstorms. It becomes very humid and is almost continually overcast. In the north the rains are also heavy.

After August the weather moves in reverse, so that by December the south is again experiencing light rain and the north drought. In the north, the wind called the *harmattan* brings dust clouds from the Sahara and makes the temperature very cold.

Northern Nigeria regularly suffers sandstorms originating from the Sahara.

9

The Benue River in the dry season, near Yola in eastern Nigeria.

RIVERS

Many of Nigeria's neighbors suffer from the yearly problem of drought and inadequate water supplies. Nigeria itself is blessed with two major river systems that provide not only irrigation for the land, but also a means of transportation.

The Niger, one of the world's longest rivers, starts in Guinea. It flows northward through Mali, providing enormous areas with irrigation water and hydroelectric power before it gets to Nigeria. In Nigeria, it replenishes the Kainji Dam to provide hydroelectric power and water for irrigation. In central Nigeria, it joins the Benue and becomes navigable, which provided a major form of transportation in the days before an adequate road system was built. The Niger flows over relatively flat land, so it is a slow-moving river. It floods regularly during the rainy season and causes enormous damage, often because whole trees caught in the flood smash into buildings or fences beside the river's bank.

The thousands of tons of soil washed down into the river during the rainy season have created the Niger Delta. This covers thousands of square miles, and makes both the river and its delta difficult to navigate because of the shallowness of the waters. Much of Nigeria's reserves of oil have been discovered in this delta area.

The Benue, which is the largest tributary of the Niger, is also fed by many smaller rivers with their sources in the highlands of the Jos Plateau. Many of these smaller rivers have been dammed, providing a steady supply of water for the surrounding population and a source of hydroelectric

FOREST WILDLIFE

Besides the hardwoods that have made the rain forest such a valuable source of income, giant bamboo and palm trees also grow in the forest. While strolling through the forest, the careful observer will notice flame-of-the-forest trees, with their striking red flowers or small white orchids growing from their branches. High up in the canopy, monkeys chatter away, and the incessant noise of cicadas and crickets fill the air. Hornbills caw overhead, and a carelessly overturned log may reveal some teeming insect life or even a snake.

Small animals still thrive here, notably tiny antelope, but you would be very lucky to come across any of the more dangerous creatures that once threatened explorers such as Mungo Park.

power for the tin mines of the Jos Plateau.

Another important waterway is the Cross River in southeastern Nigeria. Before the development of roads and railways, this river was the main thoroughfare of the Cross River State and its capital city, Calabar, a focal point for trade.

THE RAIN FOREST

Before human habitation, a belt of tropical rain forest 170 miles wide lay across southern Nigeria. It supported a massive population of wildlife, including elephants, wild boars, buffaloes, bushbucks, and leopards. Because the land has been cleared for agriculture and the valuable hardwood timber harvested, only a fraction of the forest still survives. It now supports only a tiny number of the animals it once harbored.

The remaining forest is very similar to other forests in South America and Asia. A top layer of giant trees forms a canopy. Below this, there is a second layer of trees with distinctive buttressed roots often linked by woody climbing plants. A thin layer of bush exists at ground level and, finally, low-growing herbs carpet the jungle floor. The rain forest depicted in the *Tarzan* movies, with a thick mat of vegetation that needed to be cut away in order to make a path, is fictional. These rain forests can be strolled through quite easily. The rain forest is evergreen. It provides a major source of income for the country in the export of valuable woods such as iroko, sapele, and obeche, all used in making furniture.

Guinea savanna in southern Nigeria. Here, the flora is much greener than the more desolate savanna of the north.

THE SAVANNA

The savanna covers the middle section of Nigeria. It is an arid part of the country, with months of dry weather. It is subject to the risk of accidental bush fire, as well as deliberate fires started by farmers to clear the land. The savanna is typically covered in high grasses interspersed with trees and smaller shrubs. Regular bush fires have eliminated the more delicate plants, and the tendency is for the trees to disappear as fires and firewood collectors remove them.

THE NORTHERN PLAINS

The northern plains cover a large area, beginning in the region of the Jos Plateau. Before the area was cultivated, it was covered by short grasses and hardy, thorny trees such as acacia. For half the year there is no rain, and the rivers dry up completely. Some people believe that eventually the Sahara Desert will extend to cover the northernmost parts of the plains.

THE SHADOOF

Thousands of years old, the shadoof still has a part to play in the irrigation of modern Nigeria, particularly in such areas as the Jos Plateau.

The shadoof, a water-raising device, provides a means of moving water from a source to the surrounding fields. It has a bucket at one end and a weight at the other, and is swiveled around, depositing water onto the soil.

THE JOS PLATEAU

Almost in the center of Nigeria, the Jos Plateau stands 300 to 600 yards above the surrounding plains. It is bounded on all sides by an almost sheer and very spectacular drop to the plains below. Weather on the plateau is distinctly cooler and wetter than on the surrounding plains. The area is densely populated and farmed for cash crops, including the Irish potato. The plateau has been extensively mined for tin deposits, and abandoned mines have been used for irrigation schemes using the shadoof.

KAINJI DAM

Completed in 1968, the damming of the Niger at Kainji resulted in the creation of a lake 90 miles long and, at its widest point, as much as 17 miles wide, covering 800 square miles. Forty-two thousand people were moved to make way for the dam. One hundred seventeen new villages and two new towns were built, all in an untraditional style of architecture.

The dam provides hydroelectric power, and offers the potential for much larger irrigation projects. Fishing has also increased as a local activity.

Three fishermen on Lake Chad in northeastern Nigeria.

LAKE CHAD

In the extreme north of Nigeria lies Lake Chad, whose shores Nigeria shares with Cameroon, Chad, and Niger. A very shallow lake made up of the remains of an inland sea, it shrinks to half its size during the dry season. Most of the Nigerian shore has not yet been exploited agriculturally, and it remains marshy, unused land. The lake provides fish and some minerals, as well as water for cattle grazing on its shores.

MANGROVES

The coastline of Nigeria is notable for its large areas of swampy, lagoon-filled land—similar to the jungles in adventure movies, with lianas and palms making movement difficult. Mangrove forest exists where the swampy land comes into contact with the sea. The roots of the mangrove trees are like stilts, holding the main plant out of the water, but providing anchorage for it.

Mangroves will survive in salt and tidal water, and their stilt roots not only provide for the tree but encourage large amounts of marine life such as oysters and shrimp. The seeds of the mangrove germinate while still inside the pod on the tree, putting down aerial roots into the water.

MAJOR CITIES

LAGOS Until recently, Lagos was the capital city of Nigeria. It still is the country's commercial, industrial, and cultural hub. Built on a series of islands in a lagoon, it is protected from the enormous waves of the Atlantic Ocean by a series of smaller islands

Holy Cross Cathedral and City Hall in central Lagos.

and sandbanks. The islands are connected by a number of bridges, and a railway was built earlier this century to provide trading links with the interior.

Lagos island, the original site of the city, houses government offices, major department stores, and many office blocks. A great number of people commute from the suburbs of Lagos into this area each day. Around the railway and harbor many industries have developed.

The population growth in recent years put an enormous strain on a city that was never ideally located in the first place, and its infrastructure began to crumble under the pressure. The consequence was the creation of the Federal Capital Territory and the new capital city of Abuja, still in its infancy.

15

A suburb of Ibadan.

IBADAN Like Lagos, Ibadan is in the predominantly Yoruban southern region. It spreads out over a range of hills chosen as the site because it was a location easy to defend against enemies. It was originally a walled city covering 16 square miles. By 1851, most of the inhabitants commuted daily to their farms in the surrounding countryside. Even now, Ibadan's population consists mainly of commuting farmers.

Today, all the members of an extended family live in houses close to one another (in the old days they would have been within one compound) and share the family farming land. The town's life revolves around its markets, which serve wholesalers during the early mornings, housewives during the days, and families and night owls looking for a meal during the evenings.

The city's various ethnic groups live in their own districts, with special areas set aside in the town for outsiders, such as the Hausa-Fulani, or settlers from other continents, such as the Europeans or Lebanese. Ibadan is connected to Lagos by rail and is Nigeria's second biggest city. It is congested and overcrowded, as all Nigerian cities tend to be, but it pulsates with life and vitality.

CREATING A NEW CITY—ABUJA

As the impact of the economic boom of the late 1960s and 1970s took its toll on the already fragile infrastructure of Lagos, it became obvious that satellite towns and further expansion would not solve the problem of overcrowding.

A plan was drawn up to create a new capital unlike any other city in Nigeria—fully planned with the necessary infrastructure in place before the workers arrived. The Federal Capital Territory was created in the heart of Nigeria. It has the advantage of being away from any one ethnic area, because the government hopes to set aside ethnic differences and create a unified country.

Still in its infancy, the city officially became the capital in 1991, just in time for Nigeria's expected return to democratic government.

KADUNA Once the capital of northern Nigeria, Kaduna is typical of cities in the northern states. It was planned and built in 1912, and has broad avenues, planned areas for commerce, government buildings, and staff quarters. It also has an industrial area and a railway depot conveniently close to the city center.

Centered in the cotton-growing area of Nigeria, the city has textile factories, a car assembly plant, and an oil refinery. A large proportion of the residents are connected with the Nigerian armed forces. Kaduna is also well known for its educational institutions.

Kano, northern Nigeria. The sand-colored buildings and architecture are typical of this part of Nigeria.

HISTORY

NIGERIA TODAY is a modern creation. From prehistoric times until the 19th century, the country was inhabited by a series of much smaller tribal groups. Even within tribal areas—say, for instance, the Yoruba lands—tribes fought and took slaves from each other. In the south, tribes tended to organize without any form of government or leadership, and in the north a series of jihads (holy wars) created Islamic kingdoms.

For many years, this situation suited the European countries who were exploiting the region. But after the abolition of slavery, some Europeans began to settle in the area, and it became necessary to provide a government to protect them. The British created a protectorate at the turn of this century, bringing together much of Nigeria as we know it today. For geographical and tribal reasons, the country remained divided into northern, eastern, and western Nigeria.

Opposite: **The Emir's palace in Kano. The Emirs controlled northern Nigeria before the British incursions into the area.**

Below: **A panoramic view of the old quarter of Kano, one of Nigeria's most historic cities. The city was founded in the 12th century, and was the seat of the Hausa Empire.**

HUNTER-GATHERERS

The earliest evidence of human development in Nigeria was discovered in the north of the country and dates back to the New Stone Age. Throughout northern Nigeria, pebble tools, hand axes, and cleavers made from stone have been found. The early humans who made these tools lived by hunting wild animals and gathering fruit, seeds, and roots. They were nomadic, moving on from one site to another in search of the animals that they hunted. It is also probable that they set fire to the savanna as a means of driving animals into pit traps.

THE NEOLITHIC REVOLUTION

By the Late Stone Age, about 10,000 to 15,000 years ago, humans had also begun to settle in the south of the country. The earlier development of the north may be explained by the fact that the heavily forested areas of the south were more difficult to survive in than the northern savanna.

The Late Stone Age is characterized by more settled communities that would have grown crops and kept domestic animals. Archeological sites have revealed pottery models of cattle, sheep, and goats, and remains of domestic animal bones have been discovered.

Remains of tools indicate differences between the north and the south of the country. In the south, the majority of stone tools excavated are large, heavy stone axes, and hoes. In the north, the tools are microliths—small flakes of stone with a cutting edge. This contrast can be explained by the differences in local vegetation: people living in the northern savanna needed knifelike tools to cut grass, while those in the southern forests needed heavier digging implements.

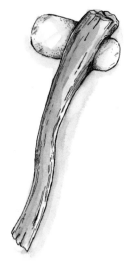

A typical heavy stone ax of the Neolithic period.

THE IRON AGE

Sites in the Jos Plateau have produced much evidence about Iron Age life in Nigeria. The Iron Age is the period when humans first learned to make iron tools. This occurred in Nigeria between the 5th and 3rd centuries B.C. Iron Age culture developed first of all in the middle belt of the country, in the humid savanna, where a large variety of crops could be grown.

The use of iron meant that more crops could be grown, as iron hoes and blades could help cut down larger trees and dig soil more effectively. The development of iron tools also indicates the potential for making weapons, and therefore the conquest of other villages.

THE NOK SCULPTURES

The original figurines that distinguish this period in Nigerian culture come from excavations around the Jos Plateau. Many of the terra cotta objects are masks or models of animals.

Besides telling us much about the degree of sophistication of the culture that could produce such beautiful figures, they also provide information about the culture itself. Some of the pottery figures carry what must be iron axes.

The models of cattle found show the particular breed that was domesticated in those times. Modern Nigerian cattle have humps; these do not. Many of the sculptures also show evidence of having been copied from wood carvings.

The northern gate of the old city of Zaria, northern Nigeria.

THE PRE-COLONIAL NORTH

The first example of a modern state in Nigeria was the Kanem-Borno civilization, which occupied Borno in the northeast of modern Nigeria. The empire gradually spread south in search of better land. Its capital was Ngazargamu.

Established by the 13th century A.D., this civilization consisted of a series of city-states. These city-states formed governments, collected taxes, and maintained armies, particularly cavalry regiments. The Kanem civilization brought Islam into Borno and eventually Hausaland. Hausaland spent several centuries as a kind of buffer area between the Kanem-Borno empire and the large Songhai empire to the west.

After the collapse of the Songhai empire, the Moslem caliphates of Hausaland and Sokoto flourished and expanded but became corrupt, losing many of their Islamic values. During this time, a wandering race of Islamic people, the Fulani, became influential and brought about a religious revival. They accused leaders of abusing power, collecting taxes illegally, practicing polytheism, and many other corrupt practices. Finally, in 1804, a jihad was launched by a Fulani leader. All over the region similar jihads prevailed, establishing a Moslem Fulani empire with Sokoto as its center.

THE FULANI STATES

Under the new Fulani caliphs, a complex social structure was built up in each settlement. The local communities were administered by men nominated by a caliph. Each community had a tax collector who collected taxes on land and farm products. Each craft guild had a head person who also collected taxes from the craft members and sent the revenues to the state capital. These were in turn spent on helping the poor, building mosques, and providing local utilities.

THE SOUTHERN STATES

The history of the southern states is clouded in myth and legend. Study of archeological sites shows that the eastern and western halves of the south followed very different patterns of civilization.

In the east, communities tended to be stateless. Settlements were very small and far apart. Leaders were, as they remained well into the 20th century, people who had shown themselves worthy of respect. There were no formal elections, just a consensus that a particular person had the right to determine the village's future.

In the west of the country, a different system developed. By the 14th century, a civilization with its capital at Ife was established, which gave rise to two more powerful states, Benin and Oyo. In the 12th century, Benin, situated deep in the rain forest, was the capital of a state that extended from the Niger to Lagos. It traded with Europeans and was visited by the Portuguese explorer d'Aveiro in 1486. Trade began with products such as pepper, but quickly moved on to slaves, beginning the boom years of the slave industry. (The city still exists, though the state has disappeared.)

Oyo, the other major state to evolve from Ife, extended its authority westward toward modern Benin (the country). Its armies were cavalry-based because it was outside the rain forest belt, where there was less of a threat to livestock from tsetse flies.

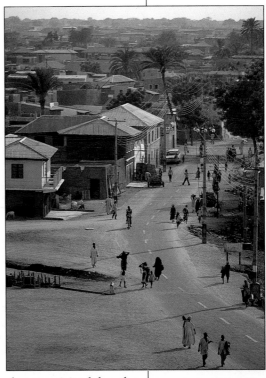

In 1804, the Fulani jihad leader, Usman dan Fodio, led a revolt against the Hausa overlords. In 1807, Kano city (above) was finally captured by the Fulani.

23

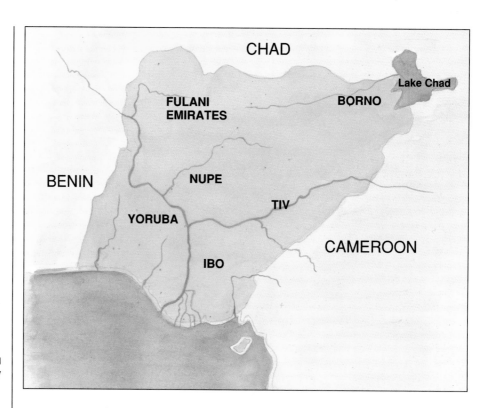

The political and tribal divisions of 19th century Nigeria.

THE 19TH CENTURY

Just about the time that the Fulani were launching their holy wars in northern Nigeria, the British decided that slavery was wrong and began enforcing their beliefs on the people who had supplied them with slaves to such lucrative effect for so many years. The ban had little effect, since the Yoruba and Fulani wars provided enormous numbers of slaves. The trade just moved westward, and the slavers learned to evade the British navy. As a consequence, the British attacked and burned Lagos in 1851, and later occupied it in 1861.

British influence increased, and by 1884, Britain had established a monopoly on the legitimate trade of the area—palm oil. British missionaries were widespread over southern Nigeria, bringing education to those who would become the administrative class of another stronghold of the British Empire. For the most part, Britain kept out of internal wars, except, of course, when it affected trade. But in 1884 Britain claimed Nigeria as its own. Yorubaland, still suffering from internal wars, was brought under control by treaty. Benin, which was still a slaving stronghold, was approached in 1897 by a British trading mission, but its troops massacred the British force. As a reprisal, the British sent a much larger and aggressive force against Benin, and the city was razed.

Small encroachments were made into Fulani territory, but were relatively unsuccessful until the area was systematically attacked using superior fire power. By 1903, Sokoto had surrendered and its sultan fled.

Being few in numbers and prone to diseases such as smallpox, diphtheria, malaria, and leprosy, the British used local rulers as their representatives. They collected taxes and used a part of the revenue to administer their areas. The once powerful Emirs became powerless, and the British governor took their place. The *zakat* tax, which had supplied the needs of the poor and infirm and provided education, was abolished, leaving no replacement for these services.

Missionaries were restricted, and so the north became underdeveloped, with education denied to its children. Existing schools were closed, and requests for textbooks were refused. By 1914, the Sokoto area had only 19 elementary schools for a population of 1.4 million.

By the end of World War II, enough Nigerians had become well traveled and educated to realize that Nigeria had a right to self-government. The British administration had effectively kept the various parts of the country isolated politically and, in providing education for the south and none for the north, had created jealousies and bitterness that have dogged the various attempts to establish democracy since Britain withdrew.

In 1946, a new constitution was established giving power to the three regions—north, west, and east—but maintaining British power in central government. Newer versions followed in 1951 and 1954, both of which strengthened regional powers against those of the central government.

British explorers traveled deep into the country in search of new profits, and many died of local diseases, giving Nigeria the name "White Man's Grave."

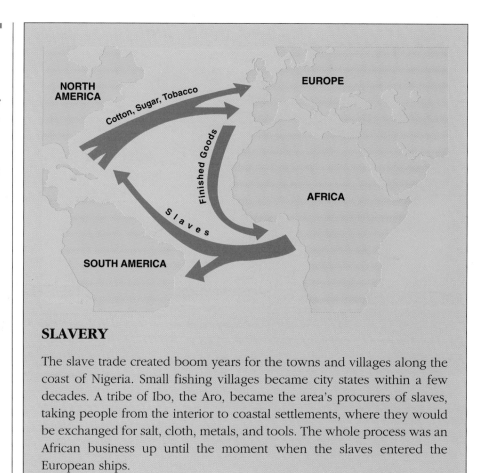

SLAVERY

The slave trade created boom years for the towns and villages along the coast of Nigeria. Small fishing villages became city states within a few decades. A tribe of Ibo, the Aro, became the area's procurers of slaves, taking people from the interior to coastal settlements, where they would be exchanged for salt, cloth, metals, and tools. The whole process was an African business up until the moment when the slaves entered the European ships.

THE BRITISH PROTECTORATE OF NIGERIA

Amalgamated into one protectorate in 1914, the south and north had little in common except their British rulers. The following 40 years saw an enormous expansion of the economy, particularly exports. The companies controlling and profiting from these exports were all British. Palm oil, peanuts, tin, cotton, cocoa, and high-quality hardwoods provided British companies with huge profits.

A railway system was established connecting Port Harcourt and Lagos with northern production areas, and roads connected these major ports with the east.

NIGERIA SINCE INDEPENDENCE

The years preceding Nigeria's independence saw the establishment of three major political parties based on regional loyalties. The British policy of denying the north proper education had resulted in its being both economically weaker and less able to take part in the central government.

Nigeria became an independent republic on October 1, 1963. A British-style constitution had been set up in 1960, but was unable to handle the strain caused by conflicting national and regional interests, and collapsed within six years. Corruption charges were followed by treason trials, then general strikes and attempted coups.

In January 1966, the constitution was abandoned and General Johnson T.U. Aguiyi-Ironsi, an Ibo, was declared the temporary head of state. He attempted to deal with regionalism by abolishing the regions. In July of the same year, Ironsi was ousted and killed, and a new supreme commander, General Yakubu Gowon, came to power.

The bustling streets of Lagos indicate Nigeria's recent social and economic advances.

THE BIAFRAN WAR (1967–70)

Meanwhile, an even more destabilizing force was growing in Nigeria. Inter-regional mistrust and rivalry had grown to the point where the Ibo, the dominant tribe of the east, were in danger of their lives. The Ibo formed the bulk of the administrative classes under colonial rule. Ibos were spread throughout Nigeria, and held many government posts.

During Ironsi's brief regime, Ibos in the north were massacred. Under Gowon, more massacres caused the eastern region to talk about secession. A general exodus of Ibo people back to their own region began. Gowon's government tried to defuse the situation by declaring 12 new states to replace the three old regions. That way, each region would be less powerful. Four days later, the eastern region announced its secession as the independent Republic of Biafra.

The Nigerian government received the backing of the West. Few African states recognized Biafra's claim to independence, since they too consisted of poorly meshed ethnic groups and could suffer the same fate of having economically powerful areas secede. Biafra held out for 30 months. Its people were driven farther and farther east into forest and swampland. Pictures of children starving to death reached the West. Many thousands died. Finally the Ibo surrendered. Gowon, instead of punishing the Ibo further, followed a policy of reconciliation, and in today's Nigeria there is little evidence of this terrible war.

POST-CIVIL WAR NIGERIA

Gowon's regime was now able to focus on the need to create a unified country. Oil revenues had spiraled upward, owing to the oil price boom of the 1970s. A massive development plan was under way, when Nigeria's third coup since independence took place. Gowon was replaced in a bloodless change by the reforming Brigadier Murtala Mohammed. A supreme military council was formed and many high-ranking officers and former heads of services were retired.

All seemed set for a period of progress when a counter-coup occurred, killing Mohammed. The coup was unsuccessful and, within a month, 32 people involved in the coup were publicly executed. The new government embarked on reforms that were to be financed by oil revenues, and began to study which form of democracy would suit Nigeria best. Finally, an American-style democracy was chosen. In 1979, Nigeria returned to civilian government, led by the northerner Shehu Usman Aliyu Shagari.

Four years later, accused of corruption and fraud, this government also gave way to another military junta, which in turn has sought a return to democracy.

Soldiers preparing for combat in the Biafran War in 1968.

GOVERNMENT

AS CAN BE SEEN from Nigeria's history, one of its major problems lies in establishing what type of government the country needs. Prior to the arrival of the European powers, there was no such country as Nigeria.

The three regions of the country, each of them torn by internal differences, were brought together as an administrative whole by the British in 1914. British policy determined that the three areas be kept isolated from one another.

As a consequence, the enormous territory that Nigeria's new government inherited in 1963 was not only diverse to the point of not being governable, but also torn by dissension, religious differences, and rivalry.

TRIBAL CONFLICT

Before the British brought railways and economic advancement, the various regions had practices that could not lead to a stable and happy community. Slavery was not invented by the Europeans. It was widespread in Nigeria before European incursions into Africa. Tribes would take slaves both from rival groups and from their own people.

In some areas, human sacrifice and cannibalism existed. Many cities still have the walls that were built to protect their citizens from attack by their immediate neighbors.

Above: **The telecommunications building on Lagos island: a visible monument to Nigeria's recent political stability.**

Opposite: **The state parliament building in Kaduna, northern Nigeria.**

31

Regional governments took charge of developing the economies of their respective states, the health of their citizens, schooling, and all direct taxes, including income tax.

CONSTITUTIONAL HISTORY

By 1951, the governing body was working to produce a constitution based on the British system so that Nigeria could govern itself. This constitution gave most power to the national government and very little to regional powers. It failed to work.

In 1954, a second constitution was created that also failed miserably, since it served regional interests and caused strife among regions.

Two military coups in 1966, one by southern generals and one by northern ones, removed the whole structure and replaced it with a supreme military council. All top government and civil posts were taken up by soldiers. State governors were also soldiers.

While being highly undesirable as a form of government, military rule controlled corruption and ensured that issues of national interest were given preference over local interests. In 1976, the military government reorganized the country into 19 states in an attempt to dissipate regional power.

RETURN TO DEMOCRACY In 1979, democracy was tried again. This time safeguards were inserted into the constitution to prevent a single region from determining government policy. The president was elected for four years and had to have a majority in at least 13 of the 19 states. The Senate and House of Representatives were directly elected for four-year terms. This way, a system very much like that of the United States was in operation, with the two houses and the presidency acting as a system of checks and balances.

Within each state, a governor was elected for a four-year term, and members of a single house of assembly also had four-year terms of office. States still retained power of taxation, but national laws took precedence over state laws, as in the United States.

The president and Senate were virtually powerless bodies, and most power resided in the House of Representatives, which was elected on the basis of population. This meant that the most highly populated areas dominated government.

There were no national political parties, just local leaders with the interests of their own state at heart. Northerners held 167 of the 312 seats, and consequently dominated parliament. Because of this, government jobs were given out unfairly, and national laws that served only the interests of one area were passed. Each region had a mini-government modeled on the one above, and its own civil service.

This second attempt at civilian government coincided with the enormous revenues generated by the oil industry. But the inherent corruption in Nigerian society resulted in the diversion of oil revenue into private citizens' hands and eventually led to the bloodless coup of 1983.

This military government was well received, and its leader, Major General Mohammad Buhari, was well respected. He was killed in a later coup that brought the present ruler, General Ibrahim Babangida, to power. Babangida has since weathered at least one attempt to remove him from office.

A *jakada*, or tax collector, representing the Emir of Kano.

HUMAN RIGHTS

Considering that it has consisted mainly of military regimes, Nigeria's record is good. However, after the coup in 1983 that ended the second attempt at democratic government, several laws were passed aimed at rooting out corruption. These included the permitting of secret military trials, the power to search homes without a warrant, and allowing detention without charge. Sentences allowed by civil courts include public execution by firing squad and flogging. In addition, those charged with crimes are assumed guilty and must prove their own innocence.

Equality of the sexes does not exist, and women who marry lose many of their individual rights. However, there is religious toleration, freedom of the press is recognized, and the right to teach and publish in the ethnic languages is respected. Within tribal groups there are still some unpleasant practices, such as child labor and physical scarring of women. Homosexual practices are banned, with a 14-year prison sentence for those convicted.

LAW AND ORDER

Under civilian law, both federal and state courts existed. The judiciary consisted of a Supreme Court and two lower courts—the Court of Appeal and the High Court.

Since the coup in 1983, the civil courts no longer have jurisdiction over charges of corruption and ruining the economy, which now are decided by military courts.

The police are organized nationally under an inspector general responsible to the military government. Each state has a police commissioner. There is also a unified prison system organized by the military government.

POLITICS AND POLITICAL PARTIES

Prior to the 1966 coups, there were three parties roughly representing the north, east, and west of the country. After the second attempt at democracy in 1979, laws were passed insisting that parties have a national basis. This worked quite successfully, with all parties rejecting regionalism.

With the return to military government in 1983, all political parties were banned. Creating new ones has been a major problem for the government of Babangida, who was expected to oversee the return to democracy in 1993.

The name "Nigeria" was coined by an English journalist, Flora Shaw, in 1897.

The headquarters of the Biafran separatists at Onitsha, on the Benue River. Since the Biafran War, successive Nigerian governments have been reluctant to encourage political and cultural diversity.

THE CENSUS

In a country divided by religious and ethnic differences, something as simple as a census becomes a highly controversial issue. Representation in parliament is based on population, and if one area is highly populated it can dominate government. A census was taken in 1963, the year Nigeria gained independence. It gave the northern, Moslem states a majority in parliament. Since it can be so important in terms of who controls the country, further census-taking attempts were abandoned, because it was in the interests of regions to cheat.

A second successful census was undertaken in 1991. There were many problems involved, the biggest being that in many households in the north, women do not leave their homes and may not be seen by strange men. The family could only be counted by female census takers.

During the census, on November 26, the country was closed to the outside world. All movement within the country was banned from 7 a.m. to 7 p.m., and a million census takers were employed. Census takers were not allowed to work in their own regions and had to work in pairs. The whole affair cost about $130 million. The result showed that the two halves of the country, north and south, are very evenly balanced, with about 44 million people in each.

THE PRESENT

Of Nigeria's eight governments since independence, six have been military ones. The present military government is committed to introducing democracy in 1993, but already the schedule is running into problems.

In 1987, General Babangida called for a two-party system to replace the confusion of small parties that existed before the coup. He created two parties, "one a little bit to the right of center, and one a little to the left." They had no leaders, but it was suggested that people should join the party they preferred and then elect leaders.

The two parties are called the Social Democrats (SD) and the National Republican Convention (NRC). They seem to have formed along lines that are national but religious in nature, the SD being the party approved of by Christians, and the NRC supported largely by Moslems. The division into north and south has been further prevented by the reorganization of Nigeria into 30 states—nine more than previously existed.

In 1991, elections were held amid widespread accusations of electoral fraud. The National Electoral Commission (NEC) was created to monitor any abuses of the system, and was given the right to ban anyone for doing so. Many people were banned. Today, criticism of the way the parties have been established is widespread, as are comments about the way that the government has funded and controlled the policies of the parties.

President Ibrahim Babangida meets African trade mission representatives.

ECONOMY

NIGERIA'S ECONOMY in the decades since independence has been compared by some critics to the finances of a lottery winner. At independence, Nigeria was an under-developed agricultural country, producing cash crops in an increasingly depressed world commodities market. By the time the civil war had started, the oil industry was providing the largest share of the country's income. During the oil boom of the 1970s, there was more income than anyone knew what to do with. Huge projects were undertaken to build roads, ports, schools, and medical facilities, and to create an educated class of technicians ready to deal with the enormous wealth.

Cash crop production fell, lots of people moved to the cities, and food and palm oil had to be imported. Soon, Nigeria was spending more foreign currency than the oil produced. Many people lined their own pockets from government revenue. One day, the bubble burst. Oil prices fell and Nigeria was in serious debt, unable to complete many of its fine plans for rebuilding the country.

Today, the situation is better. The present government has worked to rebuild other industries, and many have been set up to produce goods to replace expensive imports. Projects begun in the 1970s have been completed, including the creation of a new capital city. Nigeria may yet emerge as Africa's most powerful state.

Above: **Weighing cocoa bags.**

Opposite: **A local sub-urban store in Lagos, southwest Nigeria.**

Cotton and tobacco, two very popular cash crops for Nigerian farmers.

AGRICULTURE

About 80% of Nigerians make their living from the land, mostly as subsistence farmers who sell some cash crops to supplement their income. Food production fell as a result of the oil boom, while the population increased. The high cost of fertilizers and machinery prevented the type of farming that would make the land more productive. For a time, it was much cheaper and easier to import staples such as sugar and corn, rather than invest enough in agriculture to make the country self-sufficient.

When the slave trade came to an end in the late 19th century, palm oil became the area's most important export. It was this that motivated the British to create a colony at Lagos. The main palm oil-growing areas are in the south of the country, in a rough agriculture belt from Calabar in the east to Ibadan in the west. Much of palm oil production came from harvesting wild trees. Palm trees grow to about 30 feet, producing football-size bunches of fruit that are pressed to produce the oil. The oil is processed in Nigeria.

RUBBER

Like palm oil, this industry has been built up from the
wild rubber plants, which in the past were often destroyed
in the process of tapping rubber. During colonial times,
rubber was exported in its raw state. But more recently,
Nigeria has seen the need to develop its own processing
industry. Much of the raw material is now turned into the
finished products in Nigeria.

CASH CROPS

Nigeria has not yet fulfilled its enormous potential for the
production of cash crops. It is developing the cotton
industry again for its own use rather than for export.
Cocoa provides a small proportion of exports, and
coffee, rice, kola nuts (used in the manufacture of cola
drinks), and tobacco are produced for local markets.
Among the subsistence crops are an enormous range of
cereals and vegetables, all of which have the potential to
become major sources of income if farmed on a large
enough scale.

Cattle farming is largely practiced in the north of the
country by the nomadic Fulani people, who are being encouraged with
the aid of irrigation projects to settle down and produce cattle along more
commercial lines. Other irrigation projects have led to rice growing in the
Sokoto area, and the cultivation of wheat, rice, and cotton around the
previously unused shores of Lake Chad.

Containers are used to
carry palm oil from the
bush.

OIL

In the early years of oil production Britain, as Nigeria's colonial ruler, was the chief beneficiary of the newly discovered oil. After independence, Nigeria expanded its markets to sell to Western Europe. More recently, Japan and the United States have become Nigeria's chief markets.

By 1974, Nigeria was the world's ninth largest producer of oil, which provided 80% of the country's foreign exchange earnings. Nigeria has the advantage of being a relatively stable producer, is close to Western markets, and produces high-quality oil. At first, most of the oil companies in Nigeria were foreign-owned, with only 50% of profits going to the state. Valuable income was also lost because foreign companies chose to import the necessary skills and equipment rather than develop them locally.

Successive governments have passed legislation insisting on a higher share of the profits and the use of local workers. In the 1970s, this became almost a battle between the companies and the government, and resulted

in oil shortages and the inability to fulfil oil quotas.

In the 1980s, Nigeria exported $7 billion of oil per year, and even had trouble fulfilling the quotas. A very popular but wasteful policy of the government has been to subsidize local gasoline prices. This has resulted in huge waste and a great deal of smuggling. The future of Nigeria's oil industry is also a short-term one. Experts suggest that there is only about another 20 years of production before the oil runs dry.

STEEL

For many years, Nigeria's desire for a steel industry has been seen as a symbol of the country's shift to an industrialized economy. As a producer and processor of raw materials, Nigeria is dependent on world prices. Much of its oil wealth disappears into importing expensive foreign-built items such as machinery and cars. A steel industry would free Nigeria of an enormous economic burden.

But study after study has suggested that a steel industry would be impractical. Local deposits of iron are poor, as are those of coal. Studies by governments interested in investing in a Nigerian steel industry have repeatedly come to the same conclusion: that it is not economically feasible. Nevertheless, Babangida's government is committed to the industry, and steel is being developed at Ajaokuta.

Tie-dyed material drying in Kano, northern Nigeria.

TRADITIONAL CRAFTS

There are many traditional crafts still practiced in Nigeria that form the basis for a small but flourishing industry. In Benin, the home of some magnificent ancient bronzes, there are still guilds that control the production of iron implements and ivory, ebony, and wood carvings.

Oyo is the center for carved calabashes. These are large gourdlike fruits that are hollowed out and made into water vessels. Many of them are so strong that they can be used for boiling water.

TEXTILES Most of the Nigerian cotton crop is produced for home consumption. Most cotton cloth is produced in the state of Kaduna. The climate of the north is highly suitable for the plant, which is grown on small farms. It is very labor-intensive, because the cotton bolls have to be hand-picked. Inside the boll, the seeds are covered in a mass of white fibers that twist as they dry, allowing the threads to be spun. The cotton is made into brightly patterned cloth.

BIG INDUSTRIES

Until it is able to produce the items that it currently imports, Nigeria will always be economically dependent on other countries and have a high import bill. Processing plants exist for the materials that were traditionally exported to Europe, but the manufacturing industry is weak.

Centers of industry are Lagos, Port Harcourt, Enugu, Benin, Kano, and Kaduna. There are assembly plants for several models of cars, which brings some employment to the country, but these cars are not manufactured in Nigeria. At Kano, industries include manufacturers of beer, cigarettes, soft drinks, perfume, and soap.

THE FUTURE

Nigeria has the potential to be the agricultural leader of Africa. Its agriculture is as yet undeveloped, and suffers from the fact that many people see education and city life as a means of social mobility.

Much of the oil revenue has been squandered in expensive imports, or in lining the pockets of civil servants. The cost of building up the necessary infrastructure to allow Nigeria to grow has been enormous. All the necessary materials are in place for the rise of Nigeria as an African and world leader. The next decade will show if this takes place.

Dye pits in the north of Nigeria.

NIGERIANS

IN RECENT YEARS, Nigerian governments have seen the key to national stability in creating smaller states. The country is divided into 30 small units, and a popular joke in Nigeria is that the country won't be really happy until there is a state for each family. This gives some indication as to the ethnic diversity of Nigeria.

Superficially divided into three major ethnic groups—the Hausa-Fulani, the Ibo, and the Yoruba (the tribes of the north, east and west)—Nigeria is in fact made up of many different ethnic groups with their own languages, religions, and needs. Modern city life has complicated the issues even further, with settlements of various ethnic groups in all the major cities.

Roughly speaking, the major ethnic groups of the north are the Moslem, Hausa-speaking groups, whose main occupations are cash crop farming and cattle-rearing. They form the largest proportion of the population.

The Yoruba dominate the southwest of the country. There are about 12 million Yorubans, and they form the main population of towns such as Lagos and Ibadan. Nevertheless, the majority of the Yoruba, like the Hausa-speaking groups, are farmers, living in walled towns and commuting to their farms daily.

To the southeast, the dominant tribe is the Ibo. During colonial times, the Ibo were shown preference in administrative posts. Because of its oil fields and lack of scope for development in agriculture, the Ibo region is probably the least traditional part of Nigeria.

Above: **Taureg tribesmen, the nomads of northern Nigeria.**

Opposite: **Large ornate jewelry is very popular with Nigerian women.**

A Fulani woman carries her milk to sell in Sokoto, northwest Nigeria.

THE NORTHERN TRIBES

HAUSA A complex political system existed in the Hausa states long before the British arrived in West Africa. Even before the arrival of Islam, competition for trade with states to the north made the Hausa strong, while their lack of a writing system or shared beliefs kept them from forming a huge empire. Around them, the Songhai and Borno empires were being created, while the Hausa states remained small units.

Today, Hausa cities form the educational, commercial, social, and administrative centers for the surrounding countryside. The Hausa are primarily farmers, many of whom live in the cities and have other craft skills.

Until independence, government in the Hausa states was by family dynasties. Social status among the Hausa is based on degree of urbanization—those who can afford to live in towns have a higher status than those who stay on farms. The poorer people become clients of the richer, and in return for loans or help, offer their support in whatever way it can be given, often through voting.

FULANI No one knows the origins of the Fulani. They remain largely nomadic, driving their herds of cattle across northern Nigeria in search of grazing and water.

In the 19th century, it was the Fulani who led the jihads against corrupt Hausa governments and became rulers of the Hausa. They have a lighter skin color that is admired by the other tribes.

KANURI The Kanuri represent about 4% of the population of Nigeria. The majority live in the state of Borno, although some Kanuri also live in more southern towns and cities, and in Niger and Chad. Their culture goes back 1,000 years to the Borno Empire.

Like the Hausa, they are Moslem and have a similar system of client-patron relations. In the past this would have had a military purpose, but in modern times this means loans or work in exchange for political or financial support.

THE TIV Neither northerners nor southerners, the Tiv are a curious people, defeating the understanding of outsiders. Before independence, their political structure was unlike any other in Nigeria. They had no chiefs, no administrative structures, and no leaders that could be identified. They existed peaceably with one another because of ties of genealogy.

There are few Tiv towns, since they are traditionally a rural people. During 1991 and 1992, the Tiv nearly went to war with the neighboring Jukun people over political boundaries.

A Kanuri goatherd travels to sell his livestock.

*Nigerian women
in urban areas
generally dress in
Western style,
although they also
enjoy wearing
brightly colored
and patterned
skirts and ethnic
headscarfs.*

THE EAST

IBO The Ibo comprise as many as 200 smaller tribes. For many years of their history, these tribes fought with each other as well as took slaves from neighboring tribes. The typical Ibo settlement was tiny—2,000 people at most.

Colonized by the British later than the western states, they willingly accepted missionary education, and gradually became dispersed throughout Nigeria in administrative and craft work. Most Ibo became Christians, and were favored by the colonial power.

Their presence was deeply resented by groups who felt underprivileged, particularly in the north. In the 1960s, huge massacres of Ibo people in the north led to the migration of the tribes back to Iboland, where, for the first time, a sense of Ibo unity came into being.

Covering lands rich in oil, and with the biggest oil refinery in Nigeria, Iboland could easily have stood independently from the rest of the country.

In 1967 the Ibo seceded from Nigeria and set up the independent Republic of Biafra. But things went against them. The Nigerian government had the support of the international community. They gained no support from neighboring countries, whose governments also faced the threat of secession from disaffected tribal groups.

The suffering of the Ibo was well documented, as they slowly starved to death rather than surrender. Finally, after thousands had died, they admitted defeat. Fortunately, the government of that time was sensible enough to take no reprisals against them.

Officially, there is no prejudice against the Ibo as a result of the war, but memories of the suffering are still fresh and threaten the latest moves toward democracy.

CLOTHING

Traditional dress varies within each tribal group, but the typical Nigerian clothing of today originates from the north and reflects the pastimes of that region.

Men usually wear a floor-length robe, heavily embroidered at the front, over baggy cotton or silk drawstring pants and a skullcap, or fez. The looseness of the clothes protects against the high temperatures, and the pants allow for ease when horse-riding, the traditional means of transport and warfare in the north.

Women's garments are less fine, usually dark-colored and cover the whole body, with headgear that can be turned into a veil.

If the traditional dress of the north is Arab- and Moslem-influenced, that of the southeast is African. Typically, men wear a huge cloth worn kiltlike, wrapped around the waist and twisted into many folds. Women wear a less-full wrapper covering their hips and legs, and a blouse or cloth over their breasts.

IBIBO The Ibibo are the second-largest group in eastern Nigeria. There are about 1 million Ibibo living mostly on the western side of the Cross River. Their homeland lies south and east of Iboland and north of the coastal delta. Chief Ibibo towns are Abak and Uyo.

The method of farming used by the Ibibo is called "slash and burn." An area of jungle is cleared by cutting and burning the vegetation. It is farmed until it becomes infertile and then left fallow to revert back to jungle until it is ready to be farmed again.

Their chief cash crop is palm oil, although subsistence vegetables such as manioc, corn, cocoyams, and squash are also cultivated. With the decrease in palm oil production, many Ibibo have become migrant laborers, particularly on oil rigs. Like the Ibo, the Ibibo have only recently come to see themselves as an ethnic unit. In the past, fighting between villages was common.

PEOPLE OF THE WEST

A Yoruban man of Ibadan wearing the *aba,* which serves as a coat, overcoat, or blanket.

YORUBA There are around 12 million Yorubans living in an area of the southwest covering the Oyo, Ogun, Ondo, and Lagos states, and part of the Bendel and Kwara states. They make their living from fishing and growing cocoa, palm oil, yams, cocoyams, bananas, corn, cassava, plantain, and guinea corn.

They are predominantly town dwellers. A typical town has high walls and a ditch, with a centrally placed royal palace alongside the town market. Each large kinship group lives in a compound with a large, rectangular courtyard. Originally believers in spirits, the Yoruba have converted in almost equal numbers to Christianity and Islam.

Traditionally, the Yoruba were ruled by kings, each township having its own ruler. During the height of the slave trade, these kings declined in power to be replaced by traders with private armies. But the arrival of the British meant the kings were reinstated, as theirs was the administrative system that best suited the colonial power.

Today, the Yoruba practice polygamy. If he can afford it, a man will have many wives. All his sons will inherit his wealth equally, so it is difficult for single, wealthy dynasties to emerge.

Modern, well-educated Yorubans no longer live in the communities in which they were born. Instead, about one-fifth of them live in the bigger cities, particularly Lagos and Ibadan. They work in government administration or for companies where they earn wages rather than work as farmers. But they maintain their links with their homelands.

The poorer Yorubans depend on support from their families

YORUBA STYLE

Yorubaland has been influenced by many different cultures in its time, and Yoruban dress style reflects these influences. Christian men tended to dress like their missionary teachers. Those who converted to Islam followed a Yoruba-style Hausa dress. Over this is worn a series of silk or cotton gowns, with the final layer being a highly pleated *agbada*. This drapes from the shoulders to fall below the knees, and is made of the same cloth as the trousers. The wealthier the wearer, the more layers of clothing are worn and the more ornate the design and finish.

Yoruban women wear a skirt cloth called an *irobirin*—five yards of cloth wrapped in different patterns around the hips to drape toward one side. This is topped by a simple square-shaped blouse, and covered by another piece of cloth draped over the left shoulder. Yoruban women have traditionally worn a *gele* (head tie), which takes many different shapes according to the fashion of the time. It is said that the way a woman wears her *gele* tells you about her attitude, that is, what mood she is in, and whether it is safe to approach her or not!

to get jobs, while the rich are able to afford cars, making the journey back to the home village simple and fast.

EDO The Edo occupy the land from the city of Benin eastward to the river Niger. Like the Yoruba, the Edo are largely farmers, using the "slash and burn" style of farming to make a living out of the fragile tropical soil. Each season, a new garden is cleared out of the rain forest, and the previous one left to revert to its original state.

In Edo society even the farming jobs are sharply differentiated, with the men being responsible for the cutting and burning and the yam crop, while the women look after the other crops.

Edo is also the name of the language that the people of this area speak. A smaller group of Edo live around Benin, and are called the Bini. They are the descendants of the sophisticated civilization of Benin, ruled for hundreds of years by the Oba, the sacred ruler.

A 17th century account of Benin by a Flemish writer describes it as being five miles in circumference, with a beautiful palace at its center, and 30 large streets crossed by many smaller ones. When the British sacked Benin in 1897 as a reprisal for the massacre of a trade mission, they discovered exquisite bronzes, carved ivory tusks, and masks of great beauty and value.

LIFESTYLE

TO TRY AND GIVE a detailed account of the many styles of life in modern Nigeria would take several volumes. Nigeria, like other developing countries undergoing massive change, has been catapulted into the 20th century. Many people in the cities live in a way similar to yours or mine, shopping in supermarkets, cooking in modern kitchens, eating processed Western-style food, and relaxing at the movies or a disco. Ethnic ties still have an influence on their lives, but they live in a manner typical of people in industrialized societies, commuting to work, complaining about the traffic, and watching television in the evenings.

Other people, such as the nomadic Fulani, have a very different set of expectations and values. Their movements are determined by the rains, and their economic prosperity by the health of their cattle.

In the far north, women in the state of Borno might never leave their compounds and see no one but their husbands.

Opposite: **Making brass jewelry is extremely popular in the Benin region.**

Left: **Relaxing by the Niger River.**

A group of Ibo children in Enugu, southeast Nigeria.

BIRTH AND CHILDHOOD

Among the Moslem tribes—the Hausa, Kanuri, and Fulani—birth ceremonies are observed according to Islamic law with some ethnic additions. Hausa women stay in their husband's compound for the birth, and are ritually compelled by their kinswomen to nurse the newborn child. Following the birth of her first child, the mother goes to her parents' compound for a few days. Ritual washing of the mother takes place for some months after the birth. On the seventh day of its life, the child is named in the Moslem

PRENATAL MORTALITY

In the past, the death rate among Nigerian babies was very high, and this factor influenced the rituals surrounding the birth of a child. As in many other African communities, a big family is desired by everyone, since then the parents will be well cared for in their old age.

naming ceremony, where a ram is sacrificed. The child is breast-fed for two years and then is placed in the care of an older sister. All children live in the women's section of the compound, but when a boy is old enough to help his father in the fields, he moves to his father's living area.

The Fulani consider a child to be one year old after it is born. Until it is named, a child is considered as being without an identity and is called "it." The child's name is determined by the day on which it was born. In polygamous families, children have little contact with their father, although the sons of each wife expect to inherit from him. Kinship is with the mother's family rather than with half-brothers or sisters.

Among the Ibo people, it is traditionally believed that the newborn child is inhabited by the spirit of someone who has died. This spirit may or may not decide to stay in the new body. It is not until the child has begun to walk and talk that it is assumed that the spirit has decided to stay. The Ibo used to believe that the birth of twins was an abomination, and the mother and her children would have been driven out of the village.

At the age of ten, Fulani boys are considered old enough to herd their father's cattle.

Among the Ibo, scarring and female circumcision were once features of a girl's entry into adolescence, practices which have now fortunately fallen into disuse.

PUBERTY AND ADOLESCENCE

As children grow older, there are several significant moments for them connected with their family life. All Nigerian children tend to be drawn into adulthood at an earlier stage than their Western counterparts. In Hausa society, boys undergo circumcision at about age seven, which marks their preparation for adulthood.

A first marriage marks the move into adult life, although a boy's work in the fields might be more of a distinction in Western terms. The bride and groom do not have to be present at the marriage ceremony. Rituals surrounding the marriage last seven days, during which time the bride's skin is stained with henna, she is secluded for a time, and given the necessary instruction to prepare her for marriage. She must pretend to escape from the place of her seclusion, to show her modesty and reluctance to become a bride. No such rituals are performed if the bride or groom divorce and remarry.

Among the Fulani, circumcision marks the move into adulthood. At this time, the boy moves from the women's quarters to the area allocated to unmarried men, is given some cattle of his own, a staff, and some Koranic charms. It is traditional for young Fulani boys approaching marriageable age to ritually beat one another, so as to prove their toughness and suitability for taking on a wife.

At puberty, both boys and girls begin to learn dance steps and to flirt in the marketplace. The boys also perform a special dance and praise song, in which they list and describe the charms of the various eligible girls. This establishes the girls' ranking in terms of desirability. The girls similarly dance, until they find the youth they prefer and stop dancing by him.

THE MARKETPLACE

In Nigeria, the marketplace is the focal point of a village or town, and often the sole reason for its existence. Even today, after the massive changes brought about by Nigeria's new-found wealth, many people produce, transport, and sell their own goods. A Yoruban woman might make pots or cloth, or she might have a surplus of vegetables that she wishes to sell. The final price she gets for the products will determine how well she and her children eat, or how good their education can be, and consequently she drives a hard bargain.

In the bigger cities, whole markets exist only for the sale of one type of item. In Ibadan there is a cloth market, a soap market, a food market, and a craft market. These are in addition to the other many daily markets whose function changes as the day progresses. In the morning, the original producer or a middleman sells produce to the regular stallholders. Later, the housewives will buy from the stallholders, and later still the food hawkers will open up their stalls, catering to the local nightlife.

A market in Ibadan, western Nigeria. The market is a social center, and a place to exchange news and gossip.

THE ROLE OF WOMEN

In the country, many of the old ways still survive. In Ibo society, women traditionally leave their own villages to marry, and consequently women rarely own land. Inheritance is through the male line. In traditional Ibo culture, still practiced in many places, women process palm oil and trade in the local markets. This gives them an opportunity to sell their surplus crops and to exchange gossip and news with women from their home village.

WOMEN'S RIGHTS

As far as Western notions of sexual equality go, Nigerian women are badly off. Although Nigeria is a signatory to the Convention on Equality for Women, in effect this has little meaning. In law the principle of equality is not recognized, and there are no women in government. Women do not have social or economic equality.

Nigerian women have little sexual equality compared to their Western counterparts, and are usually economically dependent upon a man.

Most tribes have traditions that discriminate against women economically and make economic independence for them very difficult. In some tribes, unmarried women have no status (unless they are prostitutes), and no term of description or address. Married women must have their husband's consent when they apply for a passport.

In traditional Hausa society, most of the agricultural work and craft skills are undertaken by men, leaving women with domestic tasks such as weaving cotton, making blankets, and making sweets. The markets are also dominated by men, unlike in Ibo and Yoruban societies.

Single women have the option of becoming a praise singer, or a *jakadiya* (a messenger). Hausa women are the chief devotees and exponents of the cult of spirit possession.

POLYGAMY Polygamy is the norm in traditional Hausa society. The practice dates back to the time when many men died in the numerous tribal wars. Polygamy was a form of charity that offered protection to widows. Moslem law allows a man to have several wives, with the first having the greatest status. However, monogamy is becoming more common due to the spread of education and the influence of Christianity.

In the cities women have more independence. Many women are employed in light industry, more marriages are monogamous, and people see self-improvement and upward mobility as goals.

THE WOMEN'S RIOTS

Traditionally, Ibo society did not have the structure that the West associates with government. Leadership was by those who had proved their skills in other areas, and could not be inherited or canvassed for. In 1929, the colonial government taxed Ibo men on their property for the first time. It came as a bit of a shock to discover that they had to give money to a government— something they had no concept of, and had never previously needed.

When, in the following year, the same authorities began a survey of the property of women, a spontaneous resistance movement began. Unarmed and often bare-chested women marched through villages. In Calabar and Opobo, some court buildings were attacked. The government ordered troops to open fire, and on December 16, 1929, many women were killed—53 in Calabar province alone.

The riots were unsuccessful, but they led to a reorganization of the tax laws.

Country life is still based on the small-scale farm, with very little use of complex farm machinery or chemical fertilizers.

MARRIAGE

There are three forms of marriage in Nigerian society: the traditional marriage, which is held in the house of the woman; the official marriage, held in a registry office and which allows only one wife; and the religious marriage, which differs according to religion. Christian marriage is similar to that in the West, while Moslem marriage permits up to four wives.

In Yoruban marriages, the man chooses a wife from his community. If his parents approve the match, they help him assemble the bride price. The groom's family visits the bride's house with gifts, and the betrothal is made. The groom then owes duty to his future parents-in-law in terms of help in the fields. Part of the bride price is traditionally spent on buying equipment for the new home, while the rest is shared by the girl's family.

The wedding itself is a very colorful affair involving traditional music and dances. A disco and reception in a hotel might mark a wealthy city wedding. Once married, the woman owes her husband fidelity, domestic labor, and all rights regarding their children. In traditional marriages, wives and husbands remain distant, living in separate quarters, and financially independent of one another. In polygamous marriages, the wives take turns preparing meals for their husband.

FATTENING ROOMS

In pre-colonial times, the wedding was preceded in many tribes by a period of preparation and instruction for the future bride. During this time, she was kept in a "fattening room" and fed very well, so that by the time of her wedding she had gained a lot of surplus fat. This was considered to indicate a healthy state. In the fattening room, a bride's only occupation was to learn the *iria* dance styles. Her departure from the room was marked with much ceremony, by a special dress and hairstyle. In modern times, this process has become unfashionable, and seems unbelievable to many Western young women, who often diet to achieve exactly the opposite effect!

Nomadic Fulani marriages are arranged along slightly different lines. The boy and girl are often betrothed at puberty, and are of a similar age. The boy's father's representative and a witness visit the camp of the prospective bride and negotiate terms.

This is followed by a feast at the girl's camp, where a bull is slaughtered and eaten. As soon as the girl is old enough, the betrothal ceremony takes place at the girl's family camp. This time they provide the food. When the bride moves to her husband's camp, she is showered in milk, struck with the branches of the Fulani blessing tree, and threatened with a grain pestle.

The girl spends her days with her mother-in-law, while the boy continues to tend the family's herd of animals.

As soon as the girl is pregnant, she returns to her father's camp, where she stays to observe the many rites of pregnancy and childbirth. She does not return to her husband for two and a half years. They are then considered parents, and herders with their own herds and homestead.

It is not unusual for Nigerian women to get married two or three times or more.

When a man dies, his marriage is not automatically over. His wife, along with some of his property and other belongings, goes to his next brother. Usually, the woman will return to her own family, but it is not uncommon for her to move in with the brother and become his wife.

DIVORCE

This is a very common event in all types of Nigerian marriage. Many second or third wives come to their husband from another man whom they have decided to leave. If he decides to keep her, the new husband will pay back the bride price to the deserted husband.

Many women go through three, four, or more marriages during their lives. There is little conflict involved in these divorces, since the Nigerian notion of marriage is different from that in the West. Marriage is an economic and genealogical partnership rather than an emotional and social one. No stigma is attached to children of divorced parents.

THE WEDDING DRESS

As earlier described, tribes in the eastern states keep the bride secluded for some months before her wedding. Her body is oiled and she is given lots of food and little exercise, so that when she emerges from the hut on her wedding day she is fat.

For her wedding day, her hair is built up into a series of discs around her head, built over a structure of sticks into high crests and stiffened with a mixture of clay, charcoal, and palm oil. She wears a cloth covered in cowrie shells and bells, which is tied around her waist covering her hips. In more modern times, Western culture has convinced the Ibo that more of their body should be covered, and so the cloth is now suspended from under the arms. Her legs are covered in brass spirals, made and fitted by a blacksmith. These are worn only for ceremonies, and are removed afterwards. Other anklets fitted at this time remain. The ceremony also involves the presentation of a larger cloth, which is worn around her hips.

In the Niger Delta area, fattening rooms are also a tradition. The girl is secluded for 18 months, beginning at puberty. The bride wears a short cloth wrapped around the hips, usually made from expensive Indian imported silk, a blouse, and a hat made from coral beads and gold. Coral beads, bells, and other ornaments are also worn around the neck and ankles, and diagonally across the chest. Some tribes, mysteriously, get the bride to carry a red parrot feather in her mouth to keep her from talking.

CITY LIFE

Life in the cities has become very similar to that in the West, and is becoming more so as oil revenues and the influx of foreign experts bring new ideas and consumer goods. Lagos has many fine department stores, supermarkets, movie theaters, and all the other paraphernalia of city life.

Nigerian cities have a special quality of their own. They are often chaotic, with streets arranged in a disorderly, mazelike fashion, with heavy traffic congestion. There are also occasional power cuts to add to the chaos.

Enormous numbers of people have moved to the cities in search of a better life, stretching facilities to the limit. Many small industries have recently sprung up, providing citizens with factory or clerical work.

Downtown Lagos. Many foreign vehicles have been bought with Nigeria's oil revenues, and air pollution is on the increase.

Nigerian country life can be hard. This man has traveled 10 miles to cut firewood near Kano, northern Nigeria.

COUNTRY LIFE

In western Nigeria, a typical settlement is a small village with its own market. In the past, people tended to stay in large settlements for protection. More recently, it has become safer and easier to move away from the towns into smaller settlements.

A typical Yoruban village home is made from mud or clay, is rectangular, and has a courtyard surrounded by mud walls. The subsistence crops that the family eats are grown around the house. Farther away are the cash crops, which are harvested and sold in the markets, or shipped to the cities. Cooking is done outside the house in a wood-fired clay oven, or over an open fire.

Ibo settlements have always been very small. Houses are traditionally made from bamboo poles with vines binding the rectangular frame together. Clay seals up the gaps, and the roof is made from banana leaves. The houses have no windows, and can easily be missed as the surrounding bush hides them.

FAMILY LIFE

For Nigerians, the purpose of marriage is to have children to ensure the next generation of the kinship group. The more children the better has always been the belief.

A typical day in the life of a Yoruban country family would see each of the wives, perhaps two or three in number, getting up and preparing food for their own children. The husband sleeps apart from his wives so as not to show a preference for any one of them, thus avoiding conflicts. It would be the turn of one of the wives to prepare the husband's food, so the cost of feeding him is shared among the wives.

The father's day would revolve around his crops. His wives would have their own jobs, either processing palm oil if he grows it, or tending and harvesting subsistence crops. The children have to attend school. Afterwards, they would help their parents in their work, the older boys going to the father, and the girls and younger boys working with their mother.

A typical Nigerian city family.

A brilliant sunset over the Benue River. Sunset is a signal to Nigerian women to prepare their husband's meal; the women's style of burial guarantees they are reminded of this even in death!

REINCARNATION

Many eastern tribes such as the Ibo, Igede, Iyala, and Idomo believe that their souls become reincarnated into new members of their mother's or sister's family. To make sure that the reincarnation is successful, many preparations are made. They are especially aimed at ensuring that afflictions of the current life do not accompany the soul into the next one.

If a person was blind in this life, the sap of the ogbagbachiko leaf is squeezed into the eyes of the corpse, and cotton patches placed over them. If a woman was infertile, a cut would be made in the abdomen of her corpse to ensure that this does not happen again.

When a man dies, his head is turned to the east, so that he will know when the sun is rising. When a woman dies her head is turned to the west, so that in her next life she will know when the sun sets and her husband's meal needs cooking. When the grave is filled, black soil is used to cover the corpse. Red soil might bring skin blemishes in the next life.

MOSLEM FUNERALS

When a Moslem dies, the imam (Moslem official) is called, and he prays over the body of the deceased and instructs the family of the dead person in the preparation of the body. The body is washed, dressed in white, wrapped in a thick mat, and buried close to the house. The head is turned to face toward Mecca.

During the course of a funeral, it is thought that the ancestors are among the crowds at the ceremony.

FUNERALS

Among the tribes of the east, it is thought that the more music, dance, and ceremony that accompanies a funeral, the better the chance of the deceased making it into the afterlife. Consequently, being able to provide for one's own funeral was, and still is, imperative.

The amount of effort put into a funeral varies with the social status of the deceased. Women's funerals are brief affairs, with the masquerades and dances taking place at the compound of her father, not in the public meeting ground. Children and adolescents also get less ostentatious funerals. For men, the degree of ceremony is determined by wealth, age, and social status.

Respected members of the village are given very elaborate funerals. Sometimes the funeral is delayed until after the burial, in order to give the village time to prepare. Before the ceremony itself, a chicken will be sacrificed over the slit drum that is to be played. The drum will be the voice of the ancestors, and the sacrifice is said to improve its tone. A burial cloth of the deceased is placed in the meeting ground to represent his presence.

During the rituals, the eldest son breaks a pot, symbolizing the release of the deceased into the afterlife. The many dances carried out by the various social clubs of the village are followed by masquerades—the climax of the ceremony. Feasting and toasts to the deceased follow this. Finally, a diviner checks whether everything went well for the soul of the deceased, and the funeral is over.

Fulani milk sellers in northwest Nigeria. The Fulani believe in patience, forethought and modesty.

VALUES

THE HAUSA ETHOS Traditional Hausa values stress patience, fortitude in times of adversity, restraint, hard work, thrift, pride in workmanship, and good social relations. Another factor affecting people's behavior is the notion of *kunya* or shame, which compels people to conform to the norms of Hausa society.

IBO BELIEFS The Ibo are a strong-willed and aggressive people who flourished under the colonial government. Their traditional forms of government say much about their character. What government there was, acted as a series of checks and balances, preventing any one individual from assuming too much power.

> **BUYING A SHROUD**
>
> Many young people buy a cloth called an ekpe-ch'enu cloth. This will be their shroud when they die. It will be the first of many cloths wrapped around the body, and symbolizes the hard work and effort that the individual has put into his life.

Flouting of "the Fulani Way" is considered madness, and the wrongdoer can be banished from Fulani society.

In the indigenous religion, the spirits of the ancestors, *ale* (the earth), or *erosi* (a type of spirit), influence people's behavior, bringing harm to those who misbehave.

THE FULANI WAY *Laawol pulaaku,* or "the Fulani Way," means the fulfillment of a man's duties towards his elders, wives, and siblings. In practical terms, the Fulani economy is a fragile one, where the needs of the family and the herd are in a delicate balance. When times are hard, cattle may be sacrificed to pay for the needs of the family. This depletes the herd, and threatens the wealth of future generations.

In moral terms, *laawol pulaaku* calls for modesty, patience, and forethought. These qualities ensure that herds are cared for, gods are appeased, and difficulties are endured.

TWINS The Yoruba consider twins sacred, and always give them the same names—Taiwo and Kehinde. In the past, if one twin died, a wooden statue representing the dead twin would be made and placed on the family shrine.

Today, it is more common for people to have a trick photograph made, using two pictures of the living twin placed on the shrine. The Yoruba attitude toward twins is a distinct contrast to that of the Ibo, who consider twins an abomination and drive the mother from the village.

RELIGION

AS IN SO MANY other countries of the world, religion in Nigeria is as much about politics and power as it is about a system of beliefs.

Before the arrival of Islam and the much later introduction of Christianity to the country, Nigeria's tribes had a common belief in one god. This god could be approached via a variety of means, and was represented on earth by powerful spirits, which often took the form of local physical features. This "animism" meant that religious sacrifices or gestures of some kind would be made to a river, a mountain, or a tree. This can easily be understood if we consider the huge potential for good or harm a river like the Niger could have during its floods and dry spells.

Islam first came to Nigeria during the Middle Ages, when it was introduced by the trans-Sahara trading caravans. It was widely embraced in the north of the country by rulers quick to perceive the power that its administrative systems would bring. Various Moslem kings dominated the Hausa and Kano states, but a series of Fulani-led jihads re-established a purer form of Islamic law as empires became corrupt or lost sight of the Islamic way.

Christianity was a much later import to Nigeria. Missionaries followed the colonial rulers and set up schools. One condition of admission was conversion to Christianity. As the European traders gradually extended their influence from the southern coast, so the missionaries' influence followed them inland. As a result, the southern half of the country is largely Christian, with animist leanings. The north is mainly Moslem, with fewer animist leanings. This is because Islam has had more time to break down indigenous religious practices.

Above: **Fertility symbols decorate a typical Islamic house in northern Nigeria.**

Opposite: **A Lagos mosque. Islam has made considerable inroads into the predominantly Christian south of Nigeria.**

73

TIV RELIGION

The Tiv probably resisted the influx of the major religions the longest. In its original form, the Tiv religion held that a human being had three elements—body, soul (which is manifested in a person's shadow), and personality. The soul, or *jijingi*, is important because the soul goes to heaven, and is also inherited by the deceased's children.

In the Tiv system of belief, God created the world and also created *akombo* ("a-KOM-boh")—forces in nature that can help or harm people. Within the strongest and most creative individuals in each village, God placed something called *tsav* ("Sahv")—the power to manipulate these forces either for good or evil.

Consequently, people can become bewitched by a person with *tsav*. To counteract the bewitching, community elders endowed with *tsav* would combat the witch. In times gone by, this would have involved ritual human sacrifice and cannibalism.

YORUBA RELIGION

A tribal fetish (object believed to have magical powers) in Ife, southwest Nigeria.

By the 1950s, only about 13% of Yorubans professed to being followers of indigenous cults, most of them having already converted to Islam or Christianity.

Their traditional system of beliefs includes hundreds of deities associated with mythical figures or features of the landscape. Their creator is called *Olorun*. The Yoruba believe in appeasing their ancestors because they believe they can influence life from beyond the grave.

TRADITIONAL BELIEFS

Nigeria's many indigenous religions have in common the idea of a single creator, who, having created the earth and laid down its laws, gave people freedom to choose their own paths in life.

No one in Nigeria in the late 20th century can ignore modern scientific knowledge or the pressures of the larger religions, but old beliefs still have influence. These days, to get a good idea of some of the old ways, one would need to talk to an anthropologist rather than one of the tribes concerned. But elements of the old religions still exist, and have even come to influence the modern religions.

BAD SPIRITS

According to Ibo beliefs, some ancestors become evil spirits and never return to a body, but instead haunt their descendants. A bad spirit is called a *jinn*. No one can ever tell how a spirit is going to turn out. A perfectly good, kind person could turn into an evil spirit.

The bad spirit can be appeased by sacrifice, in the special place where the diseased and stillborn babies are left. If that doesn't work, the persecuted descendant can find out exactly who the ancestor is by consulting a diviner. They will then dig up the ancestor's bones and burn them, thus destroying the bad spirit.

IBO RELIGION

The Ibo gladly took to the religion of the missionaries, and no longer practice their tribal religion. Because of this, our knowledge of their original religion is based on anthropologists' accounts.

This religion does not include the notion of a supreme being. Traditional Ibo religion is polytheistic, that is, many different gods and spirits are worshiped. The ancestors are believed to be reincarnated as their descendants, but while in spirit form they have influence over the living. They are appeased by the living so that help can be sought from them in times of need. Spirits called the *erosi*, who inhabit aspects of nature, are worshiped, as is *ale* ("AH-lay")—the spirit of the earth.

A Friday afternoon in Kano. The Emir rides to the mosque to worship on the holy day.

ISLAM

Roughly half the people of Nigeria are Moslem and most live in the north of the country. Islamic practice, as it has been absorbed into native cultures, varies slightly from one tribe to another, but the essential principles of Islamic belief are adhered to.

Islam literally means "surrender to the will of Allah," and its tenets are to be found in the verses of the Koran that Moslems believe were dictated to the prophet Mohammed by God. There is a second body of writing called the Sunna, which consists of the accounts of Mohammed's work and actions by his companions.

The basic tenets of Islam were extended by the Koran into 114 units, which provide Moslems with a body of religious law covering every aspect of life, from intimate personal behavior and dietry prohibitions to criminal law. Dress is prescribed, and in the case of women the religious law dictates that they should cover all of their body, although this law is often relaxed.

The Islamic fundamentalism that has swept many parts of the world at various times had its impact on Nigeria during the 19th century jihads. The current movement, with its center in the Middle East, has had little effect on Nigeria.

Like Moslems everywhere, Nigerian Moslems attend the mosque on Fridays at noon. Prayers are led by an imam. Alms-giving usually takes the form of donations to the mosque, or gifts of food to the poor at festivals such as Ramadan. During the month of Ramadan no Moslem is to eat, drink, or engage in sex from dawn to dusk. This imposes a harsh regime on people who must get up before sunrise to eat breakfast, and not eat or drink again until dark. Wealthy Nigerian Moslems make the pilgrimage to Mecca, which gives them considerable status in society. Today, the hardship of the pilgrimage is more in the cost of the airfare than the difficulty of the journey.

Sunset over the dome of the Kano Great Mosque.

THE MALLAMI

These men are a kind of semi-official intermediate stage between the imam and ordinary Moslems. In practice, the many thousands of mallami ("ma-LAH-mee") are not full-time officials of the mosque, but operate in smaller communities. They teach what they know about the Koran and officiate at less important ceremonies.

The mallami often offer help in the form of Koranic charms for people who believe that they have been possessed by a *jinn*.

The Aladura churches and the Hausa Bori cult have acknowledged the importance of dance and music in Nigerian spiritual life.

CHRISTIANITY

Christianity came to Nigeria as early as the 17th century via Portuguese Catholic traders who first landed on the southern coast. It was an unsuccessful start, and was followed by the more successful Anglicans, who came in the company of the British traders. Anglican schools and clinics extended into Yorubaland and Ibo territory.

Other forms of Christianity directly imported were American Southern Baptists, Presbyterianism, and Methodism. Generally, the more established the denomination in England, the less traveled the church is in Nigeria, so as one travels into the interior of the country, the influence of such groups as the Seventh-Day Adventists and Jehovah's Witnesses becomes more obvious.

The problem with the missionary churches was that although they brought education and often medical assistance to the people of Nigeria, they were used by the colonial oppressors, and became identified with them in the people's eyes.

Many Nigerians who were devout Christians felt that the church was dominated by their rulers. So African churches began to come into existence. Their quarrel was not with the nature of the religion, nor its practices, but with a system which meant that most of the officials of the church were white.

African churches first came into existence in the early 19th century, increasing in number in the 20th century. For the first time, churches were run by Nigerian clergymen supported by Nigerian parishioners. Anglican religious practices were strictly adhered to, although some concessions were made to the values of polygamy and to the rhythms of Nigerian music.

The differences among many of the British churches have to do more with the manner of worship than any significant differences in faith. The Anglican churches practice the Anglican communion— a symbolic act remembering the Last Supper. Other Protestant services are more frugal affairs involving no such ritual.

By the 1960s, the nationalism that had led to the creation of the African churches had also ensured that the original missionary churches were run by Nigerian people.

In looking at local Nigerian religions, it is possible to see a very practical concern for the problems of everyday life. Spirits or ancestors are regularly called upon for help in dealing with problems, such as poor crops or ill health. The Aladura Church is a result of mixing the strengths of Christianity with some of the beliefs of Nigeria's traditional religions.

In general, Christian Nigerians choose their church according to their social class. The Anglican Church tends to attract those of the educated elite whose values are those of the West, and who see Sunday attendance at church as an expression of their civilization. The new churches tend to be a little less substantial looking, and attract poorer people—those who have more need of material help. However, many middle-class people attend both churches, preferring both the excitement and spontaneity of the new churches, and the social standing of the older ones.

Local religions closely relate to the practical problems of everyday life. Spirits will be called upon to help with work in hand.

79

Moslems praying outside the Kano Great Mosque, northern Nigeria.

NEW FORMS OF OLD RELIGIONS

While the majority of Nigerians have converted to Islam or Christianity, neither religion fits neatly into the spirit of local religions. Most important in local religions is the kinship group, whether it be the family, extended family, clan, village, or larger groups. Individual groups appeal to local deities in their own fashion for protection from, and help with, the hardships of life.

Divination and oracles play a large part in discovering exactly which spirit or ancestor has been offended, and how to deal with it. The newer religions tend to concentrate on the idea of good behavior as a condition of gaining entry to heaven, and tolerating life's problems rather than seeking divine intervention.

In the south of the country, the highly ritualized and ceremonial meetings of the Anglican Church have failed to supply a basic need of the Nigerian people, which has been filled by the Aladura churches. Aladura priests offer their congregations prophecies, protection against witchcraft (often thought to be the cause of illness), and healing. The apostolic group of Aladura churches tends to be a little more reserved, offering pastoral help rather than prophecy. Meetings are quieter. One, the Christ Apostolic Church, does not allow polygamy or any Western medicine.

The spiritual group of churches offers much more lively meetings, involving singing, drumming, dance, and street processions. Worshipers wear colorful clothes and prophets explain dreams. Spirit possession and talking in tongues is another common feature. The spiritual churches allow both polygamy and Western medicine.

All types of Aladura churches offer an emotional involvement in their meetings. They have brought into their rituals behavior inherent in local religions, things not traditionally connected with Christian churches.

THE FUSION OF ISLAM AND LOCAL RELIGIONS

We have already seen that among the Hausa local religious practices have become incorporated into Islamic beliefs in order to deal with the shortcomings in what Islam has to offer.

The Bori spirit-possession cult in particular offers help and social status to those who suffer in this earthly life. Spirit possession often involves a trancelike state in which calabashes are carried on the head signifying the spirit that has entered the medium. During the trance state, the mediums dance, prophesy, and perform feats considered remarkable by the audience. Many of the dances performed at Hausa Moslem festivals can be directly related to the old belief in an earth deity.

LANGUAGE

IT IS NOT KNOWN exactly how many languages are spoken in Nigeria. It is unrealistic to think that Hausa, Ibo, and Yoruba are the only important languages in the country. Probably somewhere around 100 languages have been or are spoken, just in the north of Nigeria. Of these, some may be about to become extinct, while others, such as Hausa, have become common, and are spoken by many northerners as a second language.

In the south the situation is just as complicated. The Ibo languages are mutually unintelligible, that is, one tribe cannot understand another, even though they have the same ancient origins.

The arrival of the British further complicated the language situation. The southern areas of the country were brought under British rule much earlier than the north, so in the south a pidgin developed based on Yoruba or Ibo grammar but using English words.

Opposite: **A Nigerian Moslem transcribes the Koran using a calabash ink pot.**

Left: **Children learning English.**

People go to a market to exchange news, as well as to buy and sell goods. The variety of different languages spoken in Nigeria means pidgin is a very popular form of communication.

SOUTHERN LANGUAGES

IBO There are over 200 Ibo tribes, but the variety of different dialects means communication between these groups is not easy. For a while, Ibo became a common language among the surrounding tribes, but this was ended by the division of their region into four states during the 1970s.

YORUBA There are 50 Yoruba kingdoms, each with its own dialect. In recent times these dialects have tended to merge. In the 1820s, a Bishop Samuel Crowther from Oyo, a Yoruba-speaking kingdom, mentioned how he could not understand the language he heard in Lagos, another Yoruba-speaking town!

Like Ibo, Yoruba became a local common language for a time, being spoken by people in rural areas near the Yoruba kingdoms. The use of English as the medium of education has brought this use of Yoruba to an end.

ENGLISH

In the past, English was the official language in the south of Nigeria, while Hausa remained the medium of communication and education in the north. In present-day Nigeria, English is the official medium of instruction in all schools, universities, and colleges. It is the language spoken in the courts and government offices, although Hausa is still officially listed as a second national language.

For many people, studying English is seen as the way to upward mobility. Families will speak their own language at home, but will switch to English in public situations. It is the language used in administrative jobs, seen by many people as secure and influential positions. It is also the means to higher education either in Nigeria or abroad.

For many years, Britain was Nigeria's chief trading partner, and so in business, English served the user well. In addition, other countries setting up businesses in Nigeria would send employees whose second language was English.

Sociologists now suggest that English has created a new social class in Nigeria consisting of people who, whatever their mother tongue, use English as a status symbol. Snobbery aside, this must be a useful element in helping create a sense of unity in the country.

TIV

Living in central Nigeria between the Benue and Katsina rivers, the Tiv number about 1 million people. They are unusual in that their customs and language are very different from all the other language groups of Nigeria.

Tiv is closer in structure to the Bantu languages of southern Africa in that there are several classifications of nouns, not just masculine and feminine.

Two Koranic scribes concentrating on the task at hand, northern Nigeria.

HAUSA

In the northern states of Nigeria, Hausa is the dominant language. Around three-tenths of the population speak Hausa, either as a first or second language. Since the Hausa have traditionally been traders, their language traveled with them wherever they went, and so the people in the neighboring states, such as Kano or Borno, use it as a common language. For a time, the Hausa empires extended as far as Yorubaland, and the language was known that far south.

Unlike the Ibo or Yoruba languages, Hausa is common to all the people who call themselves Hausa. But Hausa has been affected by the other languages it has come into contact with. About a quarter of its vocabulary is Arabic in origin, while many of the words for craft skills or institutions are of Kanuri origin.

Hausa is a tonal language, and one word can have a variety of shades of meaning, depending on the pitch and variation used when it is spoken.

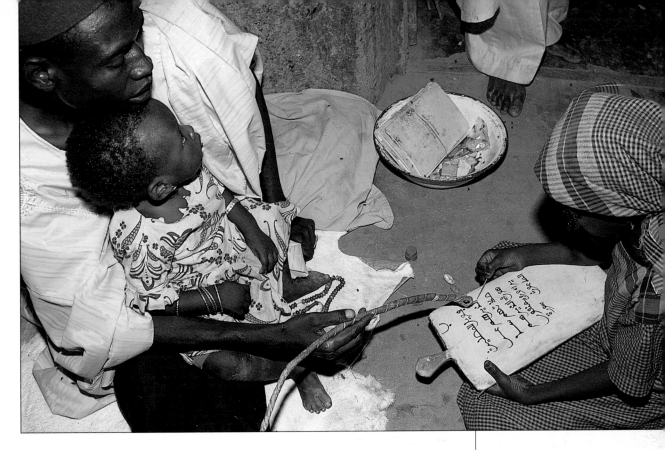

For example, the word "kashi" can mean "fighting," "rain-soaked," "heap," or "excrement," depending on the intonation, so it is important to get the tone right!

FULFULDE

Fulfulde is the language spoken by the pastoral Fulani. Today, most Fulani are settled in Hausa towns or villages, speak Hausa, and look very much like them. The pastoral Fulani are the ones who have maintained the traditional lifestyle of moving with their herds.

Fulfulde is a very distinctive language, quite unlike the other languages of northern Nigeria. It is not a language spoken only in Nigeria—Fulani nomads travel all over the Sudan, Niger, Upper Volta, and Senegal.

In each of these areas, the dialect is different, clearly affected by the languages spoken locally. Fulani, like Hausa, has adapted to local usage. The Fulani have found it necessary to speak the languages of the people whose land they depend on for cattle fodder, so most pastoral Fulani speak two or three languages.

Pidgin English allows people who have no common language, and who are from different parts of Nigeria, to communicate.

PIDGIN

In a country with hundreds of languages, some highly creative linguistic invention takes place. Most people who have an elementary education know their own language and English, and usually have at least one more language at their command.

Pidgin is a speech system that developed to enable speakers of two different languages to communicate. In Nigeria it must have begun when the European traders landed and bartered for slaves and oil. There is evidence of this origin in certain words now used in Nigerian pidgin— words such as *savvy,* from the French "savez-vous." This could well have been introduced by the French sailors who manned the ships.

The Creole languages of the West Indies probably developed from the mixture of languages spoken by West African slaves brought to the islands. It is a mistake to think that pidgin is a debased language.

Generally, pidgin in Nigeria obeys Yoruba or Ibo grammatical rules, but uses English words. It is more widely used in the south of the country where the traders first landed, and is used by uneducated people in ethnically mixed urban areas. It is also used by groups of southerners living in foreign enclaves in northern towns.

Nigerian pidgin is used in many primary schools where English has been introduced but has not yet become the medium of instruction. One might contrast this with Sierra Leone, where Krio, a pidgin language, is fast developing into an indigenous language.

A recent newspaper article in Nigeria used pidgin to express its disapproval of election violence: "We dun tire for wahallah in dis country," which means, "We are tired of political violence in this country."

CODE SWITCHING

Nigeria's wide variety of languages has led to the interesting phenomenon of "code switching"—that is, speakers switching from one language to another as they talk. This happens in all languages; the French even have a national body that attempts to keep foreign words from entering their language, but most countries are happy to accept foreign words into their national language.

In Nigeria, code switching often occurs when topics change. Two people may be talking about some domestic topic, using their own tribal language. When they move on to some more technical or international topic they will, without really noticing, change languages, probably to English. Many of the indigenous languages lack vocabulary in certain areas, so it is necessary to change languages. In other cases it might just seem proper to use the more formal language. Two people in an office might talk about their work in English, but comment on the weather in Yoruban.

Other conversations might move in and out of languages mid-sentence. Someone speaking in Yoruban, say, to another person who they feel is being too flippant, would introduce the English "you're wasting time" to make their point more forcefully. Sometimes, they might give their words added politeness by using the English forms, "please" or "thank you."

ARTS

LIKE MANY COLONIZED COUNTRIES, Nigeria has experienced tension between the demands of the local culture and those imposed by new religions and values. Traditional art has always been functional in Nigeria. For instance, dance was related to social needs, teaching, and ritual.

The arrival of Western culture has meant that many old art forms are in decline in Nigeria, no longer having a purpose. Many dances are no longer performed except in special shows, so the mask makers' jobs are disappearing. Funerals are becoming urbanized, so the elaborate tombstones and memorials of tribes such as the Ibibo are being replaced by organized city cemeteries.

Above: **A commercial pottery workshop.**

Opposite: **Handmade caps for sale in a Sokoto market. Artistic creation generally has a practical or religious purpose in Nigeria.**

Calabashes have been replaced by plastic containers. If a market still exists for the intricate leatherwork or pretty woven cotton cloth of the northern states, it is because the rich are rediscovering their roots, or because of tourist demand for such things.

The government is aware of the problem. With the resurgence of national pride, there has been an attempt to recover the old ways through such events as the All-Nigeria Festival of Arts. But this is superficial: the dances, music, and mimes performed at these festivals are just for show. They no longer fulfill their original purpose, which would have been to celebrate the harvest of yams or to initiate adolescents into adulthood. More hopeful for Nigeria are the wholly new art forms that are emerging from the old.

EARLY ART FORMS

The oldest known works of art in Nigeria are the Nok terra cotta figures, excavated from a site near the Jos Plateau. The figurines date back to 400 B.C., and were probably placed in the fields to protect the crops. From these figures, we can see that what we now classify as art had a purely practical purpose when originally created.

Closer to the idea of art for its own sake are the bronze figures and plaques of the cities of Ife and Benin. The ancient city of Ife was in Oyo province in southwest Nigeria, and was the capital of a kingdom established in the 11th century. Its artisans created bronze heads and terra cotta figures. It is probable that the figures were used in rituals in which

CONTEMPORARY NIGERIAN ART

Nigerian art suffered when the country was part of the British Empire because it was judged by Western standards. To the Western art critic, used to the idea of art as something that uplifts and instructs the beholder, Nigerian art was "primitive" and somehow needed to evolve into the sophistication of European art.

But instead, modern Nigerian artists have made use of the techniques of European art to evolve an African art. Aina Onabolu (1882–1963) and Akimola Lasekan (1916–72) used conventional European portrait styles to paint Nigerian figures, but from a Nigerian viewpoint. A contemporary artist, Ben Enwonwu, has used a variety of Western styles to evolve his own Nigerian images. His painting, "Agbogho Mmuo," is a representation of a masquerade dancer that has been praised as a visualization of rhythm in motion.

A 16th century ivory pendant from Benin. The crown is decorated with delicate carvings of European heads.

the figures of past kings would be paraded as a form of ancestor worship. The figures are naturalistic in style, and depict many details of dress and jewelry.

Benin succeeded Ife in power, and by the 16th century it had grown into a fine capital city. Bronze casting techniques were probably borrowed from Ife during the 13th century.

At its height, Benin was producing fine relief sculptures, which were used to decorate altars used in ancestral rites. The wall plaques depicted scenes from court life, historical events, and complex symbolic motifs.

The work in bronze was equaled by iron castings and ivory carvings. Today, many of these items are in museums in Britain, taken there after Benin was sacked in 1897, with many of its art treasures looted. The quality and technical skill of these works of art had an enormous influence on the European art world. The Europeans were surprised to find such fine and quality work in Africa, a place they considered primitive and undeveloped.

The art of carving still continues in the city of Benin, and it has retained its functional purpose.

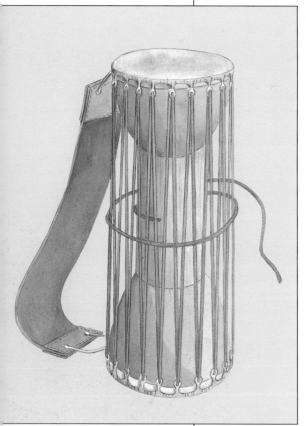

The Yoruban *dundun*, otherwise known as "the talking drum," because of the enormous range of sounds it can produce.

MUSIC

In Nigerian culture, it is difficult to make clear distinctions between music, art, and dance, since they are all inextricable parts of the whole cultural tradition. In Nigeria, religion cannot be easily distinguished from musical expression. Likewise, Nigerian music cannot be described without explaining its role in ritual and festivals in the various states.

Nigerian musical instruments vary according to tribe, but there are some common elements. Rhythm is very important to Nigerian music, and all tribes make use of various percussion instruments. The Hausa have a *kalangu*—a tension drum that is able to reproduce some of the tonal elements of the Hausa language. Similar to this is the Yoruban *dundun,* an hourglass-shaped tension drum that can vary in pitch, again reproducing the sound of spoken Yoruban. Tension drums are made from a solid piece of wood, open at the top but with animal skin stretched over it. The Ibo also have a tension drum, but in addition use a slit drum. The slit drum is made from a solid piece of wood that has been hollowed out in such a way that its two sides give different sounds when the player strikes it. Technically, it isn't a drum because it has no skin, but it is used in the same way.

Another traditional musical instrument is the xylophone, made from small pieces of wood that are struck to give out different musical notes. Other percussion instruments are gourd rattles, calabashes (for striking), thumb pianos, and harps.

But instruments are only a tiny aspect of Nigerian music. Most music includes words, sung not by an individual performer, but by the whole community taking part in a celebration or festival. The spectacle of their movements would be only a part of the whole picture, created by costume, mask, fire, figurines held above the dancers' heads, and so on.

Sakara is a Moslem Yoruba-style of music that originates from the traditional praise song of Yoruba society. Groups of musicians were paid to sing songs in praise of one particular political leader. It developed during the 1920s, and is performed by men, led by a praise singer who plays a *molo*—a two-stringed lute. The praise singer leads the song, introducing new lines of verse as they occur to him with the chorus following his lead, echoing the lines after he has sung them. It has come to be performed at all Moslem religious festivals, such as the celebration marking a pilgrim's return from Mecca, the naming ceremony, weddings, and other events.

Asiko is the Christian version of this. Its rhythms are faster, and the music consists of drums and a carpenter's saw, and sometimes bottles. Lyrics are in Yoruba or pidgin, and like the sakara songs, involve call and response.

"Highlife" is another combination of local and Western styles, this time largely Western with some local influences. It is like the brass band and ballroom type music of the 1930s and 1940s, given the added vitality of African rhythms.

A northern woman plays a one-stringed guitar.

The Ibibio dancers.

DANCE

Traditional dance is a vital part of Nigeria's social life. The various tribes use dance as a means of instruction and as an initiation into adult life. They also use it as a way of communicating with the gods and as a means of choosing a potential marriage partner.

Traditional African dance rarely takes a form that Westerners identify with dancing. Men and women rarely dance together—in fact in the early part of this century, Nigerians were shocked at the sight of Western men and women actually touching each other when they danced. Men and women dance in teams. How well a boy or girl dances might determine his or her worth as a marriage partner.

More professional dancing, for example, that done by a village association at a funeral, is performed by men wearing the carved masks and costumes associated with the appearance of a god in the village. In many cases, these dances are secret affairs, and women are banned from the meeting place when they are being performed.

MASQUERADE

An essential part of the rituals surrounding the rhythms of life in Nigeria is the masquerade, which is chiefly performed for entertainment. The masquerade has been used for purposes of war in the past. The Oynyantu masquerade dancer performs only at night, with a machete in hand and human skulls dangling from his waist. It is a sight designed to inspire courage against an enemy.

Another masquerade, again designed as a prelude to war, involves two figures: one dressed as a man in a tight body stocking and carrying a carved wooden mask, and a female wearing a large velvet costume, which is manipulated as a part of the dance.

Often the masqueraders are not telling a particular story. Individual masqueraders represent different ancestors or gods, and appear towards the end of a festival in a sudden and often frightening rush of activity. Parading masqueraders mime the actions of the deity they represent, but the actions of each one have little bearing on the actions of the other masqueraders.

For many tribes, children symbolize total innocence and purity, so some dances involve only small children or virgin girls.

WOMEN'S DANCES

Dance is not a male-dominated occupation. Among the Igede tribe of Benue State, the Imwo Association exists to regulate the behavior of women and protect their interests. Its dances often express social criticism, in particular aimed at over-aggressive males.

Another Igede women's association performs at funerals, using bamboo clapping sticks as percussion. But among the Igede, women are banned from playing drums or wearing masquerade costumes.

ANANSE, THE SPIDER GOD

One very famous set of stories originates from the Hausa people. These are the stories of the spider who was more clever than all the other animals. In one story, God sent the spider to earth to fetch something, but did not tell the spider what it was. The spider disguised himself, went back up to heaven, and was able to discover that he was to fetch the sun, the moon, and darkness. Of course, the spider was also clever enough to return to the Earth and collect them, thus proving his great skill and cunning.

Fables that teach a moral to the listener are also popular. A Yoruba story tells how the wild goat refused to help the other animals keep their pool of water clean. They got so angry with the goat that they drove it away, and it was forced ever after to live in the company of humans. This story demonstrates another purpose of storytelling: it passes on the moral standards of the tribe. This story not only teaches children to cooperate, but also offers an explanation for the existence of domestic goats.

Br'er Rabbit originates from the West African oral tradition of storytelling.

LITERATURE

Nigeria has a rich literary tradition that predates the introduction of Western culture and literacy to the country.

Nigeria's oral tradition goes back to the very origins of West African society. Its stories include creation myths, stories about the origin of individual tribes, and stories about the gods. These stories were crucial in pre-literate times, because they formed the people's means of keeping in touch with their past.

This tradition has survived both the effects of literacy and the massive disruptions of slavery and transportation to another culture and continent. Slaves from Nigeria took many of their folktales with them to other lands. In the United States for example, the stories of Br'er Rabbit have their origins in Nigerian oral tradition.

MODERN LITERATURE In modern literature, Wole Soyinka is probably the most famous Nigerian writer. He was born in 1934 near Abeokuta, attended Ibadan University, and then Leeds University in Britain. He worked for a time in English theater. He is well known for his strong opposition to apartheid and military government.

His works were banned for a period, and he spent time in jail during the Biafran war after his efforts to mediate between the warring parties failed. He was awarded the Nobel prize for literature in 1986. He is perhaps most famous for plays such as *A Dance in the Forest, The Lion and the Jewel,* and *The Swamp Dwellers.*

Another well known Nigerian writer is Chinua Achebe, whose famous novel, *Things Fall Apart,* is a regular topic in school literature examinations. His novels deal with the problems of social disintegration caused by the massive changes sweeping Nigerian society. Other novelists have taken up similar themes, including Cyprian Ekwensi and Festur Iya, the latter in his excellent novel *Violence.*

In 1991, the British Booker prize was won by another Nigerian author, Ben Okri, for his novel *The Famished Road.*

Theater is equally rich. Besides the plays of Wole Soyinka written in English, playwrights such as Fela Davies, Comish Ekiye, and Zulu Sofola write in both English and pidgin. In the Yoruban tradition, the Ogunde theater founded by Chief Herbert Ogunde has evolved. It is an operatic form of stage play that combines Yoruba stories, dance, and music.

Wole Soyinka, Nigeria's most distinguished man of letters.

FILM

Nigeria has a flourishing film industry. Calpenny Productions, a Nigerian film company owned by Francis Oladele, produced Nigeria's first major feature film in 1971, *Kongsi's Harvest*. It was based on the novel by Wole Soyinka, who also acted in the film. Other films made by the same company are *Bullfrog in the Sun*, a joint venture with the then West Germany and the United States. The first film in one of the indigenous languages was *Amadi*, a 1975 film made in Ibo.

In the Yoruban language, *Ajani-Ogun* incorporated aspects of Yoruban theater into the medium of film, for the first time suggesting a completely new direction for Nigerian film-making. Other films made in the same idiom have been *Black Goddess*, a Portuguese language co-production with Brazil, *Orun Mooru,* and *Money Power*.

The Emir's palace at Kano. The architecture is typical of northern Nigeria.

DOMESTIC ARCHITECTURE

The Nigerian climate varies from intensely hot, humid, rainy weather, to overcast and dry, to near desertlike conditions. The architecture of the country likewise reflects the various needs of people living in a variety of climates.

For centuries, the Ijo people of the Niger Delta have lived in an environment of open creeks and mangrove swamp, with very little dry land. Their response to this has been to build homes inspired by the mangroves among which they live. The houses are built on stilts over the water, and travel is by canoe, which often doubles as a mobile home when the family has a long journey to make. Wood from the ekki tree provides the load-bearing timbers of the house that are sunk into the river bed. On this is built a platform of the same wood, with bamboo walls. The roof is made from the raffia palm. The whole outer layer of the house allows the fumes, heat, and smoke from inside to escape easily.

Just as the Ijo people's homes reflect their environment, so the Yoruban settlements reflect their way of life. The city is dominated by the Oba's (the Yoruban king) palace, the neighborhood chief's house dominates the local square, and family courtyards are dominated by the quarters of the head

of the household. Like a set of Chinese boxes, the arrangement of city, neighborhood, and home illustrates the social hierarchy of Yoruban life. The traditional Yoruban house is made from mud bricks and is thatched with bamboo. Inside the courtyard, the roofs overhang to provide shady rainproof shelter for cooking, chatting, and avoiding the afternoon sun.

Ibo architecture is different again, and reflects the different nature of Ibo society. Houses are built in clusters rather than in extended family compounds. One central interior column supports the roof, with a series of exterior columns assisting. The walls are made of earth. Men's and women's houses are separate, and designed to suit their function. The man's house has an inner room and an outer room, the latter designed for receiving guests.

In the north, the houses of Sokoto are built entirely from mud. They look like large beehives, open at the top during the dry season and thatched during the wet season. The open hole at the top serves as a window, ventilator, and chimney.

LEISURE

MANY OF THE THINGS that we might call leisure actually have a more significant meaning to Nigerians. Dancing is not only for pleasure, but is a community activity that marks certain key moments in the life of a village. Similarly, in a society with no written language, storytelling is a means of passing on knowledge.

SPORT

In the towns and cities, Nigerian school children have learned to play Western-type sports, and happily take part in them. Soccer is a very popular sport, although for most people only as spectators.

More traditional sporting activities revolved around the need for men to be fit and agile, and ready for warfare when the time came.

Many of the tribal dances aimed at precision in movement and increased fitness for the participants. The war masquerades used to have a purpose of increasing and testing physical fitness and courage.

Among the Hausa, physical exercise reflects Moslem beliefs in the holiness of strength. The wrestling and boxing games that young men take part in are relics of a much older religion than Islam, based on fertility cults. In the boxing matches, two young men bind their right hands and try to knock out their opponent.

Above: **Athletes file out to rapturous applause at the beginning of a competition.**

Opposite: **A Nigerian potter.**

The popular board game Yorubans call *ayo*, also found in many other African countries in a variety of similar forms.

STORYTELLING

Nigeria has a very strong oral tradition. Stories are told on formal occasions, when whole histories are recited and accompanied by music and dance. Each night in the women's quarters family groups sit around and tell tales of their history, or moral tales to illustrate some preferred behavior. All Nigerian languages have proverbs that illustrate the way people think and behave, and these proverbs are illustrated in their tales.

In Ibo society two types of tales are typically told. One concerns the history of the particular village, how it came into being, and who is related to whom. The other type of story corresponds to the English fairy tale, and is usually a children's tale whose characters are animals or rivers, the moon or the sun.

The Ibo have a huge repertoire of proverbs, which they call on whenever they want to illustrate or comment upon some event. A game often played by the Ibo is the pairing of proverbs. One proverb is spoken, and one of a similar meaning has to be found and told by the other player.

The Hausa have as many, if not more, proverbs. "Even the great River Niger must go round an island" points out that power has its limits. *Zomo ba ya kamuwa daga zaune*—"A hare is not caught by sitting down," illustrates the Hausa respect for hard work, while "Before you tie up a hyena, think how you are going to let it go" suggests their cautiousness. The Hausa have a set of stories that they call dilemma tales. The stories have no ending, but they ask listeners what they would do or what judgment they would make under the same circumstances.

The Yoruba also have many stories about their creation myths. Here is one of them:

THE CREATION OF THE LAND Before the Earth existed, one of the gods, Odudwa, went to the highest god of all and asked him for instructions. The god told Odudwa to get some chameleons, some chickens, and many chains. Then he gave Odudwa some sand, tied him to heaven by the chains, and lowered him down to the Earth. There was no land to step onto, so Odudwa sprinkled the sand onto the sea. Then he put down a chameleon and it delicately picked its way across, one foot at a time. Then the hens landed safely. Finally Odudwa went down to live on Earth.

The other gods joined him one at a time, first the god of wealth, then the other gods. Because of his bravery, Odudwa became the most important of the gods. And ever after, the chameleon has walked delicately across the Earth.

A DILEMMA TALE

A certain man called Afik was very proud and jealous of the one possession he had—his wife. He followed her everywhere to make sure that no one else went near her. His behavior annoyed the people of the town, and so the town chief decided that Afik needed to be taught a lesson. He offered a horse, a cloak, and 100,000 cowrie shells to anyone who could shame Afik by spending some time with his wife in Afik's sight.

Musa, a clever man, had an idea. He took a seed case from a baobab tree and replaced the seeds with pieces of gold. He showed it to Afik, and let Afik persuade him to show where the tree was. Afik, of course, took his wife with him. When they got to the tree, Afik went up the ladder that they had brought with them. When he wasn't looking, Musa pulled down the ladder, and right in front of Afik's eyes grabbed his wife and started kissing her. Then laughing, he walked off to claim his prize. Afik's wife put the ladder back, but as he was climbing down, the ladder slipped, and he and the ladder fell on his wife, who was killed by the blow.

Who should be blamed for her death? Afik, because of his jealousy? Musa, for his plan to shame Afik and his wife? Or the chief, for offering the reward in the first place?

RESTFUL PURSUITS

Because of their grueling day's work, many Nigerians like to pursue restful activities in their leisure time. Television is a common item in most city households, as well as in the richer village homes. Since 1976, all TV stations have been run by the government. Many Western soap operas are enjoyed by Nigerian fans, who perhaps see the glitter of life in Dallas as something that their oil income might bring them.

Radio stations exist in all the major cities, broadcasting in English as well as 16 Nigerian languages. Voice of America, BBC World

A child in the north of Nigeria playing with a baby camel.

Service, and German and Russian stations—all produce material for Nigeria, often in one of the indigenous languages. A thriving national press exists, and has managed to survive the changes of Nigeria's fluctuating political scene. Some of the newspapers are government-owned; others are independent. There have been as many as 40 English language newspapers at one time in Nigeria. Currently, there is little censorship of the press, although there has been in the past.

The Hausa have a saying—"Give a stranger water and listen to the news," which illustrates another Nigerian activity, that is, exchanging news. Visitors to Nigeria will find that people love to listen to stories from around the world, and especially stories about other parts of Nigeria.

Children's pastimes include meeting with friends in the evening after the day's work is done, or practicing one of the many team dances performed at the harvest festival or at a wedding.

In the cities of the north people lead a more traditional life, and are less likely to spend their leisure in discos or nightclubs.

LEISURE IN THE CITIES

In the cities of the south, a middle-class elite live alongside the very poor. The atmosphere in Lagos and Ibadan is cosmopolitan, and Western-type discos and bars abound. The two popular local forms of music are to be found in the shabby bars around the marketplaces and in the sophisticated nightclubs frequented by the rich.

Highlife music is the Nigerian version of Western big-band sound, and has evolved in more recent times into a much more African-sounding music. More emphasis is placed on rhythm than melody, and the *ekwe*, a local percussion instrument, is increasingly being used, rather than trumpets or saxophones. The music is still full of social satire, rather like the similar West Indian calypso music. *Juju* music uses guitars of a Western origin, but their effect is similar to that of the Yoruba rhythms. Popular *juju* performers are Sunny Ade and Shina Peters. I.K. Dairowho, another well known performer, has had streets named after him in Lagos and Ibadan.

VILLAGE SOCIETIES

In the villages of Nigeria, many societies exist with a variety of purposes. Some societies are aimed at the betterment of the group and their families, while others represent certain age grades in the village. A member of an age grade can call on his peer group for help, and it is the responsibility of the peer group to provide the correct funeral rites when he dies.

Many of these societies are secret, have secret handshakes and codes, and have secrets that they tell only to their members. In the old days, membership in the group might require an act of bravery such as killing a wild animal. This is no longer possible, so the societies claim high entry fees. The societies seek to advance the fortunes of their members by helping them attain positions of power, and in turn increase the power and influence of the society.

In Ibo villages, societies operate as a credit association, forcing members to save and making loans when necessary.

Two members of a village society gather to discuss society business.

FESTIVALS

NIGERIA HAS MANY LOCAL FESTIVALS that date back to the time before the arrival of the major religions, and which are still occasions for masquerades and dance. The local festivals cover an enormous range of events, from harvest festivals and betrothal festivals, to the investing of a new chief and funerals. It seems odd to Western ways of thinking to see a funeral as something to be celebrated. But for many of the tribes, death means joining the ancestors, and so the deceased must get a good send-off.

The dances that were once performed by members of each village have now been taken over by professional troupes, who tour villages performing at each local festival.

The Moslem year revolves around the three major festivals, Id Al Fitri, Id Al Kabir, and Id Al Maulud. The main event in the Moslem calendar is the festival that celebrates the end of Ramadan. Ramadan is a month-long observation of fasting. During the hours of sunlight no one must eat or drink; some very religious people will not even swallow. Each evening at dusk is a celebration of sorts, as the family prepares to break the fast. In towns people do so by going out to one of the markets, where stallholders will be prepared for the hungry people. At the end of Ramadan there is a celebration, which varies in style among the different Moslem tribes.

The Christian calendar is also celebrated, chiefly in the south of the country. Christian groups have moved closer to the rituals of their indigenous religions when celebrating Christian festivals.

Above: **Yam harvesters en route to a yam festival.**

Opposite: **A masquerade dancer performing at a festival.**

ARGUNGUN FISHING FESTIVAL

One festival that has its roots firmly in modern times is the Argungun Fishing Festival, held for several days during February and March near Sokoto. The festival marks the end of the growing season and the harvest. A mile of the Argungun river is protected throughout the year, so that the fish will be plentiful for this 45-minute fishing frenzy.

About 5,000 men take part, armed with hand nets and a large gourd. During the allotted time, they fight for the fish in the river. Nile perch weighing up to 140 pounds are pulled out of the river, and the biggest are offered to the local Emirs who organize the festival. This festival began in the 1930s and has captured the nation's interest. It now includes many other events, such as canoe races and diving competitions.

YORUBA FESTIVALS

Among the Yoruba, the indigenous religions have largely given way to Christianity and Islam, but the old festivals are still observed. The traditional leaders of the Yoruba are the Obas, who live in palaces and used to govern along with a council of ministers. The Obas' position is now mainly honorary, and their chief role is during the observance of the festivals.

The Yoruban festivals honor their pantheon of gods and mark the installation of a new Oba. The Engungun festival, which honors the ancestors, lasts 24 days. Each day, a different Engungun in the person of a masked dancer dances through the town, possessed by one of the ancestors. On the last day, a priest goes to the shrine of the ancestors and sacrifices animals, pouring the blood on the shrine. The sacrifices are collected, and they become the food for the feast that is to follow.

This particular design of cloth is used for festivals relating to children and fertility.

THE SHANGO

The Shango festival celebrates the god of thunder, an ancestor who is said to have hanged himself. Lasting about 20 days, sacrifices are made at the shrine of the god, in the compound of the hereditary priest. On the final day, the priest becomes possessed by the god and gains magical powers. He eats fire and swallows gunpowder. The procession again goes off to the Oba's palace and the feast begins, accompanied by palm wine, roast meat, and more dancing.

In the past, the priest of this cult would have been a very rich and powerful man. With the decline in power of the Obas, and the large numbers of people who no longer profess to believe in the old pantheon of gods, the priests of the Yoruba are much poorer and less powerful than they once were.

THE BENIN FESTIVAL OF IROVBODE

This ceremony takes place at the end of the rainy season, after the harvest has been gathered. It is partly a kind of harvest festival but also serves another purpose—the eligible young men and women of the village are displayed before each other to be ritually acquainted.

The festival occurs only every four years, and only the very wealthy can afford to have their children take part in the ceremony. But the whole village takes part in the festival atmosphere.

In the past, the young girls who took part in the festival traditionally wore no clothing, but in modern times this type of nudity is frowned upon.

The chief parts of the girls' display are the numerous heavy armlets and leg ornaments that they wear. They are so heavy that the girls must hold their arms over their heads during the entire festival, in order to support the weight of them. Their hair is intricately plaited with coral beads.

Both boys and girls have elaborate markings painted on their bodies. The boys also take part in a tug of war.

THE IBO CELEBRATION OF ONITSHA IVORIES

In the past, Ibo society centered on subsistence farming, so few Ibo people became wealthy. Power in Ibo communities was based on the good standing of the man, rather than the extent of his wealth. But in more recent times, social status and wealth have become more important to the Ibo. While many of the old traditions are dying out, the Onitsha Ivories Festivals are becoming more common.

The title of ivory holder can be claimed by any woman who has collected enough ivory and coral to fit herself out in the costume. Usually, these women are the wives of rich men, or women who have become successful in business and can buy their own ivory.

The woman has to have two huge pieces of ivory, one for each leg. The pieces have been known to weigh up to 56 pounds each. In addition, two large pieces must adorn the wrists. Hundreds of dollars worth of coral and gold necklaces are also worn. Once she has accumulated all this, the woman must finance a feast for as many people as possible. A special priest carries out a purification ceremony for the ivories.

The next stage of the process is even more elaborate. A woman with a full set of ivories can take the title of *Ozo*. In addition to her ivories, the elaborate and expensive embroidered white gown, and coral and gold ornaments, the woman must acquire an ivory trumpet and a horsetail switch.

Men can also take this title. When a ceremony for a new *Ozo* takes place, all the similarly titled women dress up in their ivories and attend the celebration to mark the occasion.

Far left: **A man wearing an Epa mask. The Epa festival is to worship the spirits of the ancestors. Nigerians believe that these spirits enter into the masks as the men are dancing.**

OTHER FESTIVALS Many communities, including those in the north, have a version of the harvest festival. In the south, this is often a new yam festival, celebrated when the first of the season's yams are ready to eat.

The tribes that live in the Niger Delta hold the Ikwerre, Kalabari, and Okrika festivals, to celebrate the water spirits of their region. The masqueraders wear carved head dresses that imitate the heads of fish or water birds. Typically, a festival begins with a divination by the priest of the deity concerned. This is followed by ritual sacrifices, then a song and dance performance depicting aspects of the deity. The climax of the festival is usually a masquerader appearing disguised as the deity.

FOOD

UNTIL VERY RECENTLY, Nigeria was self-sufficient in food, no small matter for the largest population on a continent where food shortages are frequent. As we saw in the chapter on economics, the oil boom has had both good and bad consequences for Nigeria. One of the bad effects has been to make it dependent on expensive imported food items such as milk, wheat, and sugar. This is particularly surprising, since all these items could easily be produced in Nigeria.

Urbanization has resulted in the expansion of traditional foods and in the traditional ways of cooking being supplemented by the influence of Western culture. In the cities, supermarkets sell Western canned, packaged, and processed goods. This means that the commuter going home from work can pop into a store and buy a TV dinner or frozen lasagna, or a hamburger to take out.

Going into one of the many fine air-conditioned restaurants, one will see apron-wearing waiters delicately flicking crumbs from checkered or white linen table cloths. Their clients linger over French, Italian, Chinese, or Indian cuisine, and sip their chilled Californian wine or gin and tonic. All of this has a price, of course, that only the wealthy can afford.

Food staples vary according to region. In the tropical south of the country, subsistence crops are yams, cocoyams, and sweet potatoes. These are root vegetables and form the basis of the typical meal. Many other plants grow in the south, including rice, plantain, bananas, papayas, and pineapples.

Cattle bred and farmed in the north of Nigeria are sold and slaughtered in the south. A recent change in eating habits has seen Nigerian palates switching from palm oil to the more expensive peanut oil. This is possible due to the increased wealth of those living in the cities and because of the availability of northern oil in southern markets.

Opposite: **In the market a man sells potatoes, a regular staple of the Nigerian diet.**

FOOD OF THE SOUTH

A typical Yoruban meal consists of two dishes. One is a starchy dough, made from corn or guinea corn, or mashed vegetables. This is served with the basic Yoruban stew made from a base of palm oil, in which are cooked chilies, goatmeat, chicken or some wild animal flesh, tomatoes, and whatever green vegetables might be available. The whole dish is flavored with onion and bitterleaf leaves, and thickened with ground nuts such as agbono nuts. The meal is finished off with some of the plentiful fruit that grows in the area. Another Yoruban dish is *gari* ("GA-ree"), made from the pounded roots of the cassava plant, which are boiled or fried.

The typical range of foods available to the Ibo includes cassava, cocoyam, and edo, a kind of potato. Some corn, pumpkins, beans, okra, and peanuts are also eaten. Coconuts, oranges, mangoes, bananas, plantains, and papayas provide vitamins and sweeten the diet. Rice is also eaten, but is not a large part of the diet.

The diet of the nomadic Fulani is based on milk and whatever grains they can buy from the areas they trade with.

A RECIPE: *MASAH*

To make *masah*, a kind of pancake, dissolve two teaspoons of dried yeast in 6 fluid ounces of warm water. Allow it to stand until it becomes frothy. Mix it with 1 pound of corn meal flour until of dripping consistency. Allow it to rise for 30 minutes. Heat a tablespoon of oil in a small frying pan, so that it covers the bottom of the pan. Drop a spoonful of the batter into the pan and fry slowly, turning once. Do not allow the cake to burn. Cook all the batter in the same way, and serve on a plate with wild honey. Enjoy your meal!

THE TIV DIET Yam forms the basis of the main Tiv meal of the day—
peeled, boiled, and pounded until it can be made into a loaf. The diner
breaks off a piece of the loaf, rolls it into a ball, molds it until it becomes
spoon shaped, and dips it into a sauce. Similar loaves are made from millet
and sorghum.

The sauce consists of any meat available, plus green vegetables and oil
(usually palm oil). Typical of Tiv cooking is the use of sesame as a spice.

DRINKS Some of Nigeria's first light industries were breweries and soft
drink factories. Drinks based on the kola nut are popular, as is beer.

Palm wine, made in the south, is the drink that has given rise to the
name of a style of music born in the clubs of Lagos, where the wine is sold.
Palm wine can be fermented into an even stronger drink similar to gin.
Alcohol is forbidden in the Moslem religion, although one of the largest
breweries is at Kano, in the Moslem northern region.

Fish is very popular in the northeast, especially on the shores of Lake Chad.

THE NORTHERN DIET

In the north, the basis of a traditional Hausa meal is ground grains such as millet, sorghum, and corn. These are boiled into a porridge called *tuwo* that is eaten with a sauce made from onions, tomatoes and okra, and flavored with meat. Meat is less prominent in Hausa cooking than in the south of the country, and is reserved for special occasions.

Whereas the oil used for cooking in the south is traditionally palm oil, peanut oil is more common in the north. Cattle are kept in the more wealthy households, while the chief source of beef and milk for most people comes from trade with the pastoral Fulani. Honey, sugarcane, and kola nuts are used as the basis for drinks.

The Fulani nowadays are largely settled and work as herders for the wealthier Hausa, but their diet is based on milk and whatever grains they buy from the areas they trade with. They rarely eat meat, since this would mean unnecessary slaughter of cattle.

KITCHENS AND COOKING UTENSILS

Few other countries in the world have such a variety of ways to cook one's daily meal.

The pastoral Fulani's kitchen consists of what can be carried by the pack oxen: a receptacle for milk such as a calabash, an earthenware pot for cooking cereals, and an iron tripod to balance the pot over the fire. When the family is settled in one of its camps, an open fire in the women's quarters of the compound becomes the kitchen.

In traditional Hausa homes, the cooking area is in a covered porch in the women's section. Each wife has her own kitchen, usually a cooking place with an open fire. In the towns, there is a piped water supply. But in more rural areas, a well in the courtyard, or even a communal well outside, provides the family's water supply. Most water outside the larger towns is not suitable for drinking.

In Yoruban settlements, the same kind of arrangement applies. Cooking is done in the open courtyard unless the weather is bad. Then it is done inside, with the smoke filtering out through the spaces in the roof rather than a chimney.

These are the types of kitchens found in villages or small towns. They are also typical of the kitchens of the relatively low-paid workers in the larger towns. In the wealthier suburbs of the cities, microwave ovens, dishwashers, and food processors line the walls of high-tech, streamlined kitchens.

A woman pounding the root of a cassava plant to make *gari*.

KOLA NUTS

These are the source of the soft drinks so popular in the West. Cola drinks are made from the nut of the kola fruit. The fruit is like a large grapefruit and grows on trees. When it has fully ripened, the green skin peels away, revealing the silver and pink nuts beneath.

The nuts are crushed to produce the juice used in cola drinks. Nigerians chew the nuts to quench their thirst. The nut contains a mild, alcoholic stimulant. To give someone a kola nut is a sign of friendship.

TABOOS, CUSTOMS, AND ETIQUETTE

In traditional Nigerian dining, there are no utensils. Food is served in straw baskets and eaten with the fingers. In practice, plastic and metal utensils are imported and sold in all the markets; and in towns, the better-off use Western-style china and knives and forks. In the villages, a mixture of traditional implements and more modern ones are used.

Nigerian etiquette requires that elders be served first, and only after they

have finished are the other members of the family allowed to take what food is left. This has given rise to a popular proverb—"The elder who eats all his food will carry his load by himself."

BUYING THE GROCERIES

The market is a vital part of Nigerian life for many reasons. Whereas in the West, the direct relationship between consumer and producer is gone, replaced by huge marketing businesses, in Nigeria, the small market is still where most people buy essential foodstuffs.

In the larger cities, supermarkets exist chiefly to sell the processed food that has become a status symbol for the rich, but very few housewives buy this. The marketplace still beckons as the best place to get the freshest, cheapest vegetables and to hear the local gossip at the same time.

With modernization and better road transportation, Nigerians are no longer limited to what can be grown locally. In the past, there was little beef available in the south because cattle could not be raised there, because of the prevalence of the tsetse fly, which carries the trypanosomiasis (sleeping sickness) disease. Cattle are both carriers of the disease, which can spread to humans, as well as victims.

For the Fulani, cattle are a sign of wealth and status, and guarantee the wealth of their children. So cattle are eaten only as a last resort.

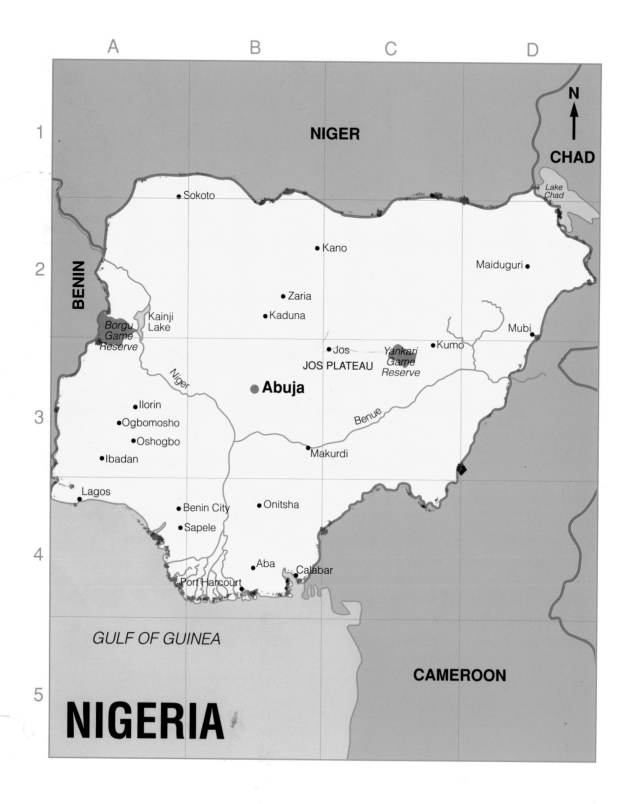

Aba B4	Ibadan A3	Maiduguri D2	Sapele A4
Abuja B3	Ilorin A3	Makurdi B3	Sokoto A1
		Mubi D2	
Benin A2	Jos C3		Yankari Game
Benin City A4	Jos Plateau B3	Niger C1	Reserve C3
Benue River C3		Niger River A3	
Borgu Game Reserve A2	Kaduna B2		Zaria B2
	Kainji Lake A2	Ogbomosho A3	
Calabar B4	Kano B2	Onitsha B4	
Cameroon C5	Kumo C3	Oshogbo A3	
Chad D1			
	Lagos A4	Port Harcourt B4	
Gulf of Guinea A5	Lake Chad D1		

— International Boundary

— State Boundary

▲ Mountain

● Capital

● City

〜 River

▮ Lake

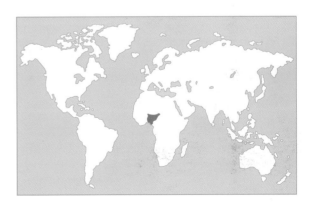

QUICK NOTES

LAND AREA
356,669 square miles

POPULATION
88.5 million

STATES
Abia Adaawa, Abuja, Akwa Ibom, Anambra, Bauchi, Benue, Borno, Cross River, Delta, Edo, Enugu, Imo, Jigawa, Kaduna, Kano, Katsina, Kebbi, Kogi, Kwara, Lagos, Niger, Ogun, Ondo, Osun, Oyo, Plateau, Rivers, Sokoto, Taraba, Yobe

CAPITAL
Abuja

MAJOR RIVERS
Niger, Benue, Cross

MAJOR LAKES
Lake Chad, Kainji Lake

HIGHEST POINT
Jos Plateau, Dimlang Peak

NATIONAL LANGUAGES
English (official), Hausa, Ibo, Yoruba, Fulfulde, Kanuri, plus hundreds of other indigenous languages

MAJOR RELIGIONS
Islam, Christianity, animism, ancestor worship

CURRENCY
Naira (21 naira = $1)

MAIN EXPORTS
Oil, peanuts, palm oil, rubber, cocoa, tin

IMPORTANT ANNIVERSARIES
October 1—National Day

POLITICAL LEADERS
'Zik' (Nnamdi Azikiwe). First president of the Republic of Nigeria.

General Yakubu Gowon. Led the country through the Biafran War. Ousted in a bloodless coup in 1975.

Brigadier Gen. Murtala Mohammed. Replaced Gowon. Assassinated 1976. Led a massive purge of corrupt elements in government.

Shehu Shagari. Elected president of the Second Republic, 1979.

General Ibrahim Babangida (current military leader). Came to power in 1983. Committed to a return to democratic government in 1993.

GLOSSARY

akombo	A Tiv word, meaning spirits that can do good or harm.
Hausa Bori	The spirit possession cult practiced by some Hausa people.
calabash	A pot made from a dried gourd. Can also be used as a percussion instrument.
Engunun	The spirit of a Yoruban ancestor who enters the body of the masquerader at Yoruban festivals.
gari	("GA-ree") A flour made from ground cassava root.
jihad	Islamic word meaning holy war.
jinn	An evil spirit.
kola nuts	Nuts of the kola tree used for making soft drinks.
kunya	The Hausa word for shame, a guiding concept in adherence to Hausa religion and culture.
Oba	A Yoruban king, once considered divine, whose power is now largely ceremonial.
Shango	The Yoruban god of thunder.
tsav	("Sahv") The magical ability to manipulate a Tiv spirit—the *akombo*.
zakat	Hausa religious tax collected by the mallami and used to help the poor.

BIBLIOGRAPHY

Achebe, Chinua. *Things Fall Apart,* Heinemann, London, 1958.

Kingsley, Mary. *Travels in West Africa*, Everyman Classics, London, 1987.

Soyinka, Wole. *The Interpreters*, Penguin, London, 1965.

The Lonely Planet Guide to West Africa, Lonely Planet Publications, Melbourne, 1991.

INDEX

PICTURE CREDITS
Victor Englebert: 4, 9, 17, 23, 44, 49,
    51, 82, 95, 107, 108, 109
R.J. Harrison-Church: 5, 7, 8, 10, 12,
    13, 16, 19, 22, 28, 30, 31, 33, 36,
    40, 42, 43, 45, 48, 56, 57, 66, 70,
    73, 84, 86, 89, 90, 91, 92, 101,
    111, 122, 123
Hutchison Library: 37, 103, 110, 112,
    116
Interfoto: 29, 35
Bjorn Klingwall: 14, 15, 27, 59, 74,
    76, 80, 83, 87, 120, 125
Alfred Ko/PRO(file): 1, 63, 79
Life File: 38, 39, 41, 46, 54, 60, 65,
    67, 72, 96, 102, 113, 119
Tony Stone/PRO(file): 6, 68
The Image Bank: 18, 47, 55, 77, 100
Val Wilmer: 99